YOUR FUTURE IN THE PERFORMING ARTS

YOUR FUTURE IN THE PERFORMING ARTS

By
GLENN LONEY
with
LAWRENCE S. EPSTEIN

RICHARDS ROSEN PRESS, INC.
New York, New York 10010

Published in 1980 by Richards Rosen Press, Inc.
29 East 21st Street, New York, N.Y. 10010

Second Printing 1982
Library of Congress Cataloging in Publication Data

Loney, Glenn Meredith, 1928–
Your future in the performing arts.

(Careers in depth)
SUMMARY: Describes the work of performers, technicians, and managers in the performing arts and discusses the qualities necessary for such careers, how to train one's talents, and how to begin a career.
1. Performing arts—Vocational guidance.
[1. Performing arts—Vocational guidance.
2. Vocational guidance] I. Epstein, Lawrence, joint author. II. Title.
PN1580.L6 790.2'02373 80–12938
ISBN 0–8239–0511–X

Manufactured in the United States of America

Because this book is intended to be helpful to students, we want to dedicate it to our mothers, Marion Loney and Shirley Epstein, who as teachers spent years being helpful to students.

About the Authors

GLENN LONEY, like producer/director Harold Prince, became interested in the theatre as a child, listening to the Metropolitan Opera broadcasts. Even in elementary school, he wrote, directed, and acted in plays. In college—the University of California at Berkeley—he was in charge of theatre lighting staff and later worked as a stage carpenter. At the University of Wisconsin and at Stanford University, where he earned MA and PhD degrees, he apprenticed in both the artistic and technical areas of theatre. Currently, he is senior professor of theatre at Brooklyn College, and also a professor in the City University of New York Graduate Center PhD Theatre Program in Manhattan. He taught and studied theatre in Europe, Africa, and the Middle East for four years with the University of Maryland. Almost every summer from 1956 to the present, he has reported on major European theatre and music festivals for such publications as *Theatre Crafts, Dance, Opera News, Reporter,* New York *Times, Christian Science Monitor,* Los Angeles *Times, Life, Ballet News, Dance-Scope, After Dark, Cue, Players, Smithsonian, Educational Theatre Journal,* and others. He is a member of many theatre-oriented scholarly and activist societies. In New York he is a member of the Drama Desk, New Drama Forum, and Outer Critics Circle.

LAWRENCE S. EPSTEIN became interested in the performing arts in the New York City public schools. In elementary school he was a band member and in high school he worked on the stage crew and played clarinet and saxophone in the school band. He received a BA in Speech/Theatre from Long Island University, having appeared in college productions and worked backstage. After serving in the U.S.

Army and working in television, radio, and community and Off Off Broadway theatre, he returned to graduate school at Brooklyn College and received an MFA in Performing Arts Administration. While completing graduate work he served internships with the New York State Council on the Arts, the Forty-Second Theatre Row Administrative Office, and the Third World Institute of Theatre Arts Studies of La Mama Experimental Theatre. Recently, he helped to organize an Off Off Broadway theatre company composed of Vietnam veterans. This small company has received funding from the National Endowment for the Arts and will produce its first season in 1979–80. Mr. Epstein is also a PhD candidate in theatre at the Graduate Center of the City University of New York and is an Assistant Lecturer at City College of CUNY. He is a Captain in the U.S. Army Reserve. He is also an avid roller skater; while in California he skated at the Roller Derby Training Center and took part in games with the Roller Derby All Stars.

Contents

Preface

When someone asks, "How can I break into show business?" it's difficult to give a simple, useful answer. Especially when the person seems to have the idea that the world of the performing arts is some kind of fortified territory that you have to break into by force. It's easier to answer someone who asks, "How could I begin studying for a career in the theatre?" But the answer still is not a simple one. Before one answers that question, he wants to be sure the person asking him is aware of just what is involved in such a career. Perhaps he ought to say, "Yes, I can tell you about some first steps in working in the theatre, but are you *sure* that is what you want to do with your life?"

In high school and college, as well as evening school, students often ask about careers in dance, opera, concerts, theatre, and even cabaret. Some teachers and counselors are familiar with one aspect of the performing arts, but few are experts on all the facets of performance. Unfortunately, although some books are available that give helpful information on theatre careers, they tend to focus on performance, ignoring technology and arts management as career areas. Some are only concerned with preparing students for careers as actors.

This book has been created to cover a fairly wide spectrum of careers in the performing arts. It is intended to give a basic background for those who are interested in considering careers in the world of opera, theatre, concerts, and dance. Obviously, books have been written to describe specific aspects of career training—such as a text on training the voice for opera singing. This brief book cannot hope to be so comprehensive, but it can tell you something about the various kinds of work that performers, technicians, and managers do in the performing arts. It can tell you about some of the qualities you may need for such careers. It can tell you about ways in which you can begin to train your talents. It can suggest ways in which you can begin your career.

An important part of this book is the Appendix. There you will find useful lists of the various unions, agents, producing organizations, professional schools, performing arts contests and awards, and other events, groups, places, and people who can help you get started in the performing arts.

Opportunities for theatre, music, and dance performers to work in films and radio/TV broadcasting are also mentioned in this book, but they are not given separate chapters or even treated in any detail. This is not because the authors wish to make an arbitrary distinction between live performance and recorded or transmitted performance. When you work in such media as film and television, the circumstances of your performance may be somewhat different from what they would be inside the frame of a proscenium stage—with a live audience watching—but you are still performing live, whether it is for a camera or a recording microphone. The problem, given the necessary brevity of this book, is that there is just too much to write about careers in television and cinema to do them justice in addition to what is already discussed. Careers in those media require another book.

The authors are grateful to all the people working in the performing arts who helped them, in one way or another, to gather and organize the information provided in this book. Working as a contributing editor for such performing arts publications as *Dance, Theatre Crafts,* and *Opera News* has been an invaluable background experience for one of the authors. Working in performance management has been just as valuable to the other. Special thanks are due—and gladly given—to Stephen Langley, director of the Brooklyn College Program in Performing Arts Management, whose own interest and dedication, as well as his impressive text on management, have been an inspiration. Equal thanks are warmly rendered to William Boswell, of the Brooklyn College School of Performing Arts Music Faculty. His knowledge of the problems involved in preparing for careers in music has been especially helpful.

And, of course, the authors are deeply grateful to Ruth Rosen, of Richards Rosen Press, for her encouragement and aid in making this book possible—and available to those who we very much hope will become the performing artists, technicians, and management experts of tomorrow.

GLENN LONEY
LAWRENCE S. EPSTEIN

YOUR FUTURE IN THE PERFORMING ARTS

CHAPTER I

Your Career in the Performing Arts

Fifty years ago there was a rage in the film industry to star cute little kiddies in cute motion pictures. In show business there is an older belief that audiences have soft hearts for children and animals. If your play or movie is in trouble, just put in a couple of adorable children, a kitten, a puppy, and maybe a comical nanny goat. The public will love it. Your play, your film will be saved.

One of the most famous of these child stars of the 1930's was Shirley Temple. Perhaps you have seen her on television in reruns of her old films such as *Little Miss Marker* or *The Little Colonel*? Blond, curly-haired Shirley Temple, with her dimples and childish talk, was adored all over America. Mothers named newborn girl babies "Shirley." They dressed their little girls like Shirley. There were Shirley Temple dolls and Shirley Temple toys.

Being a star—even before you are ten years old—not only means a kind of fame and lots of fans. It also means that you make a lot of money. But there is danger ahead as well. When you become a teen-ager, will your fans still love you? Will directors still want you to act for them? What if you never knew how to act at all? What if your popularity came only from your being cute?

Shirley Temple was, in fact, more than just a cute little girl. She was intelligent, hard-working, disciplined, and quick to learn. Those are qualities not everyone has, though they can be developed. So when Shirley Temple began to pass through what some adults like to call the "awkward age," on her way to becoming a young woman, she was still an effective, experienced performer. She had learned a lot from actual work on films. She had also been given very good training in acting, dancing, and singing. She was coached on posture, movement, diction, what clothes to wear, and how to wear them.

As a teen-ager, Shirley Temple made some interesting films. But her old fans, it seemed, could not get used to the idea that the cute little girl was really growing up. So, eventually, she retired from film-making. She was already a legend, with a name and a fame that have not been forgotten by those who loved her films. After becoming Mrs. Charles Black and raising a family, she returned to public life to serve the United States in the United Nations and abroad as Ambassador to Ghana. Her courage and intelligence have won her new, younger fans for her work for our country. She has also shown that women can do an ambassador's job just as well as men.

But there were other child stars of the 1930's, and for some of them things did not work out so well. In some cases, growing up meant the abrupt end of a film career. Disappointment. Tragedy. The public is fickle. Maybe you have already seen that in yourself. One week you like some television star, another week you are bored by him. People tend to resist change, too. If they love a child star, they don't want to see that child grow up. Some of the forgotten child actors had other problems as well. Their entire appeal was based on a lisp, a pair of dimples, or some physical feature. They never really learned how to perform, how to act, dance, sing. So when they stopped being cute, they had no real performance skills to sustain them.

Not only in the 1930's, but now as well, there is the phenomenon of the "stage mother." When Shirley Temple was at the height of her success, mothers from all over America traveled to Hollywood with their own little girls, dressed up and coached to act like another Shirley Temple. What they did not understand was that in motion pictures directors and producers are always looking for something new, something wonderful, something to make the public want to buy tickets. What they do not want—usually—is an imitation of something that is already successful. Of course, there are always producers who will try to make money by imitating someone else's plots, styles, and performers. But few careers have been founded on looking or acting like a popular star. That has certainly been proven by the number of mediocre imitators of Elvis Presley.

Studying Yourself

Of course it seems a wonderful idea to make thousands of dollars as a film star. If you are growing up and there never is enough money for all the things you would like to have or do, to earn over a million dollars for starring in a film—as Steve McQueen does—may seem like the perfect answer to your problem. But it would be an unrealistic answer. Few performers can ever command that kind of money. When they do, it may be the result of years and years of hard work, learning their craft as performers. Such monetary success may also be the result of the public's admiration or affection for a star. *She* has a pretty face and an attractive figure. *He* is muscular, tanned, and has a sexy smile. But the physical qualities that make some stars very successful often have nothing to do with talent or training.

If you are dreaming of such success, wake up! Your chances are almost nil of being discovered for the stage, films, or television purely on the basis of good looks, attractive body, or because your friends tell you you are a lot like John Travolta or Ali McGraw. Such fantasies may make you feel good, but if you waste too much time on them, they can only bring you disappointment.

To make a real career in the performing arts—if you think that is what you want to do—it is essential to begin by taking a long, careful look at yourself. Be completely, even painfully honest. That isn't easy to do. Many people go through life fooling themselves about their abilities and potentials. But when their fantasies come up against other people's realities, it is often embarrassingly obvious that they have been lying to themselves. They don't have the talent, the training, the skills that are expected of true professionals. When they are confronted with their own inadequacy, in the face of someone else's competence, they become hurt, angry, bitter, even defeated.

This need not happen to you. It will not happen to you, whatever trade, skill, position, or profession you choose in life, if you learn to study yourself and your potentials as honestly as possible. Once you have done this, you then need to relate what you have found out about yourself to the options open to you. You may, for instance, be a well-trained tap dancer, but that skill won't earn a living for you if no one is hiring tap dancers at the moment. At another time, however, you may find yourself in demand as a tap-dancing expert. This means that the process of studying yourself in relation to the world of work around you isn't something you do only when you are in your teens. When you are trying to prepare yourself in school and in part-time or summer jobs for an adult career, self-analysis is really valuable. But it remains valuable the rest of your working life. Many people in middle age complain of being "stuck" in a job or profession, of not being able to "get ahead," of being bored by what they do.

The reasons for such attitudes are varied, often complex. At the root of many complaints, however, is the sad fact that the complainer is doing something for which he has no real aptitude, insufficient training—or too much training, and often no interest. He is the wrong person in the wrong job in the wrong place at the wrong time. Many people in such unfortunate situations, if you ask them how they got there, will tell you: "I don't know. I just drifted into it, I guess." And such people are usually the last to see that things will never improve or change for them until *they* come to understand themselves and do something positive to: (1) find a job that matches their talents and training; (2) get the training necessary to succeed in their present job or a more desirable position; and (3) change their attitude about the work they are doing and the way they are doing it. For some people, an intelligent change of attitude—often getting rid of unreal fantasies about their abilities—has made all the difference on the job. What was formerly seen as drudgery becomes an exciting challenge.

In the performing arts, you do not have to be beautiful, well built, brilliant, or amazingly creative to have a satisfying career. But that does not mean your career in the performing arts will necessarily be that of a performer. And even if you do become a performer, there is no guarantee that you will become a star and make millions of dollars. In fact, the odds are very much against it. You could, instead, become an actor living close to the center of the theatre, film, and television industries in New York City or Los Angeles—and still spend part of each year unemployed. If you believe you have talent and you are able to get effective training as an actor, in your school or privately, there is also no guarantee that you will find any work, especially steady work.

But that is no reason, if you really believe you have something special to offer as an actor, a singer, dancer, musician, designer, or director, that you should not try. If you have inventoried your qualities, abilities, and skills and you think you have what it takes to succeed, then you ought to try. Even if you think you aren't handsome or beautiful, that is no reason for not trying acting if you are attracted to it as a career. Beauty, it is often said, is only skin-deep, but that is not really true. Often it comes from your *belief* in yourself. Not: "Oh, I'm so homely. Nobody likes me." Instead: "I like myself. I respect myself. I have talents I want to share with others. What I don't know, I'm willing to learn. I want to relate well to other people. If I like them, they will come to like me!"

Your belief in yourself should be based on what you know to be true about yourself—not on some impossible daydreams or fantasies. As you prepare for a career and as you pursue it, you should always stay in touch with who you are at that moment. Don't be afraid to stand back from youself and take a really hard look from time to time. Who *are* you? *What* are you doing? How *well* are you doing it? Are there any *changes* you'd like to make in your work, your training, your environment, your attitude, your life-style? How can you best make them, assuming that they will help you live a better life?

It's not easy at any time to be honest about ourselves, who we are, what our talents may be, and where we are going in our lives. If you have never tried to do that before, or if you have always accepted the evaluations of your parents, your teachers, or your friends, it won't be easy. A good way of beginning, however, is to seek the advice of a school psychologist or a guidance counselor who really wants to help you. Such trained professionals have a variety of techniques for helping you learn to size yourself up. Preference tests, tests of verbal and mathematical skills, and other testing devices can reveal much. But so can thoughtful, friendly talks with capable adults who have your best interests at heart.

Some may tell you that the performing arts are not for you, that seeking a career on stage, in films, or in television is a ticket to starvation. There are two things to consider, if this happens. One is that you should follow the advice of Harold Prince, one of Broadway's best-known director/producers. Once, when Prince was talking to a class of teen-agers interested in performance careers, he received a lot of complaints about how hard it would be to learn to sing, to master many kinds of dance steps, to earn money for the endless lessons a performer needs. Students objected to long hours of rehearsal, to the strict discipline of the stage.

Listening to all this whining, Prince shook his head. Then he said: "If anything can keep you out of the theatre, let it!"

You do not *have* to be a star. No one is *forcing* you to become a singer.

The other very important thing to consider is that there are many jobs in the performing arts that do not involve performing at all. For the star to be a success, there has to be a mass of people supporting that performance in various ways: set designers, dressmakers, makeup artists, hair stylists, recording specialists, lighting technicians, stage carpenters, painters, photographers, violinists, welders, box-office cashiers, librarians, typists, file clerks.

You may wonder how a typist could have a career in the performing arts. But who was it, after all, who typed the script from which Faye Dunaway learns her lines? If a producer such as Dino Di Laurentiis is going to offer a star such as Dustin Hoffman a million dollars and a share of the profits to make a film for him, who is going to type the letter making the offer? Or the contract Hoffman may sign? Almost every kind of occupation is needed, at some level, in the production of films and television programs. The living theatre, opera, dance, and musical concerts are more restricted, but they still require many kinds of talents, crafts, and skills.

Of course, you could be a typist at Prudential Insurance. But if you really are interested in the performing arts and would like to work with and for them, why not be a typist for Paramount Pictures? It's still typing, but what you will be typing and your work environment will be much more interesting to you than working in an insurance office. You know you may never be a star, but you want to be near the excitement and glamour of the stars? Then why not train for some position or craft you can do really well—and do it in the performing arts? Even if you become a typist/file clerk/receptionist/messenger for a community theatre group, you are involved in the performing arts. You will find you are part of a "family" of creative people, dedicated to enriching American life.

In this book, you will be introduced to the various performing arts: theatre, opera, music, and dance, as well as to the important support areas of technical theatre and performing arts management—to which the typists belong. You will discover the wide range of career possibilities, the talents and skills that are needed, and the kind of training and preparation you should begin making, even now, if you want to work in the performing arts when you finish school. None of this is set down in great detail; that would have taken four volumes or more. Instead, the purpose of these career surveys is to give you a broad general idea of what is involved in each area. Then you can see more clearly which ones might be right for you, given talent, training, and hard work. Even if you believe, after an honest self-evaluation, that you have no special talents, that doesn't rule out a career in the performing arts at some level in some kind of work. Sincerity, lively curiosity, energy, helpfulness, and plain hard work can be much more valuable to you, in the long run, than a real talent that is vain or lazy.

The most wonderful thing that can happen to you—especially in the performing arts—is that dedication and hard work often pay off in ways you could never expect or predict. If you keep on the job, working and learning, you may discover after a while that you have developed an unknown talent. Or some capable director or writer may spot a skill, an ability in you that you never were aware of. And even if you are only a typist, you might be so accurate, so speedy, so discreet, and so thoughtful that a famous director or playwright or star might ask you to become his private secretary. Imagine yourself on location with a film company in Spain! Or Japan!

It could happen to you!

CHAPTER II

Your Career in the Theatre

Theatre, as a performance form, goes back at least 2,500 years in time. In 534 B.C., so records tell us, there was theatre in ancient Athens. The origins of dramatic and dance performances, however, are shrouded in the mists of unrecorded history. One thing is certain: wanting to perform for others is a very old human urge. The earliest theatrical events on record, the Greek tragedies and comedies in the Theatre of Dionysus at the foot of the Acropolis in Athens, mingled elements of acting, singing, and dancing. Thus, the performance of music and dance is also an ancient tradition—probably older than theatre.

This section surveys the careers possible in the modern theatre, in the various ways in which it is produced. Performance careers in opera, dance, and music are outlined in a separate section, with cross references to those theatre arts and crafts that are common to all these arts. Of course, with some adjustments, theatre acting skills can be used in films and on television. But the possibilities for making performing arts careers in those media are so diverse—in technology and management as well—that only a separate book can do them justice.

Not so long ago, it was the custom to divide theatre activity neatly into two categories: professional and amateur. Originally, of course, the word *amateur* meant a lover—in this case, a lover of theatre. As it is most often used today, however, it means someone who likes working in the theatre but who has little or no training and who does it as a hobby, not as a means of earning a living.

That use of the word can be misleading. All over America, there are hundreds of club or community theatre groups involving thousands of people in their productions. Some of these groups are primarily interested in having a good time, in sharing the fun with their neighbors. Others, although they show no profits at the box office and are not full-time operations, have semiprofessional standards of performance and production. But the amateur actors are not paid. In some cases, these semiprofessional theatres may hire one or more technical people to supervise sets, costumes, and lights, or even an artistic director to stage shows and give the theatre a sense of purpose or coherence in its program. Salaries may be paid from member donations, box-office receipts, contributions from local businesses, or from city or county funds. This latter method is justified by viewing theatre as a kind of community recreational activity, which puts directors and technicians on the same basis as park supervisors or playground recreation directors. Whatever the reason may be for paying the salaries, at least they are being paid in more and more communities. Not only does that mean a better quality of theatre for local citizens, but it also means that more career opportunities are opening up in theatre. Instead of going off to New York or Hollywood—and to possible heartbreak—you may be able to stay in your own home town and work as a theatre professional.

In what is generally regarded as the real professional theatre, where artists and technicians alike are supposed to be paid a living wage, there are also some separate categories. The most obvious distinction in the professional theatre is that made between the commercial, or profit-making, enterprise and theatre companies which stress that they are nonprofit. The center of America's commercial theatre is, of course, in New York City. If it's not actually *on* Broadway, which is a synonym for the commercial theatre, it's nearby. Concentrated in midtown Manhattan, roughly from 41st Street to 53rd Street, and from Sixth to Eighth Avenues, theatres controlled by the Shubert interests, the Nederlanders, and other owner/producers house most of America's commercial successes. Commercial tours of Broadway shows still travel around the United States. But this "road," as it is called, has been greatly reduced in the last three decades. Rising costs of transportation, razing of theatres, the inroads of television on the potential audience: all of these are given as reasons the road has grown shorter. Sometimes a New York producer discovers a commercial production in a city such as Los Angeles and arranges to bring it to New York.

Today, however, the risks are so great that few producers would try to create a commercial show just for Houston or Seattle. Unless there is the prospect of performances on the road and a run in New York City, the show probably cannot hope to repay the producer the investment made to mount it, even if it is an artistic success in Houston. There is a big difference between a play's being an artistic success, which means that the critics liked it, and being a financial success, which means that the public liked it, a lot!

In New York there has also been another category of commercial theatre venture, not Broadway, but Off Broadway. Originally, it came into being as an alternative to costly Broadway productions. When Broadway shows were costing $150,000 to produce, early Off Broadway plays were being staged for as little as $6,000. Because the plays were done in theatres limited to audiences of 299, the fees and salaries paid to union performers and technicians were limited to take that reduced earning power into account. The intimacy of such theatres has also been valuable for some plays that are so small-scale that they would have been lost in a Broadway theatre.

Now, however, a Broadway musical can cost $1.5 million to stage, and an Off Broadway show can easily spend $60,000. That means, given the limited seating and the difficulty of raising ticket prices too steeply Off Broadway, that such a show has to be very popular and run a long time to show even a modest profit. On or Off Broadway, that is becoming the rule. A long run of a hit musical, such as the Prince/Wheeler/Sondheim *A Little Night Music,* is no longer a guarantee of big profits to the "angels" who invest in Broadway shows.

In New York City, this situation has encouraged the development of a third category of professional theatre. At least most of it aspires to be professional, but it is not commercial. This is the Off-Off Broadway theatre. At present, the Off-Off Broadway Association (OOBA) figures that there are well over 150 such theatre groups in New York. Owing to agreements worked out with Actors' Equity, it is possible for an OOBA theatre to rehearse and perform a play for a three-week "showcase" run. Frequently, actors may be paid only their transportation and possibly their lunches. Some OOBA theatres, such as the Manhattan Theatre Club, when they can raise the money through grants, donations, and subscription ticket sales, do pay performers Off Broadway salaries.

You might well wonder why an actor would be willing, for no more than a handful of subway tokens, to spend weeks in rehearsal of an often difficult classic or new script that will be seen only for three weeks. The reasons are various. Actors, like dancers, need to exercise, to "work out." Rehearsing and performing help fill that need. If an actor isn't working in one of these showcases, he could very well be spending his own money to do scene study with a private teacher. In an OOBA theatre, he frequently has the chance to work with admired directors such as Alan Schneider, Marshall Mason, and Lynne Meadow.

There is also the possibility that the production, if it is praised by the critics and sold out to the audiences, may be taken up by a commercial producer and transferred to Broadway or Off Broadway. Hugh Leonard's nostalgic play about his youth, *Da,* had been rejected by every Broadway producer. It was given a showcase production by Craig Anderson at the tiny Hudson Guild Theatre. The critics raved. The audience flocked to see it. Moved to Broadway, it won *seven* Tony awards. Even if a production doesn't move, being in it, designing it, or directing it shows off one's abilities to advantage to producers out shopping for talent. And then there's the fact that in New York City, there are over 9,500 Equity members, all competing for a very limited number of jobs. Who wouldn't welcome a chance to act, rather than sit at home with nothing to do at all? (In the entire U.S., there are approximately 27,000 Equity card holders.)

Fortunately for actors—and actresses—there are other kinds of commercial theatre. Nor are they limited to New York City, Chicago, and Los Angeles. A popular form of theatre entertainment that can be found all over the United States, even in some smaller communities now, is that of the dinner theatre. Audiences buy tickets that entitle them not only to watch the performance but also to enjoy an all-you-can-eat buffet or a meal served by waiters and waitresses. Usually dinner is over by the time the show begins. But if you are a sensitive performer who thought you would create great art on stage, the sound of clinking coffee cups and cocktail glasses may depress you. Still, if you are cast in a "package" show, you may find you are working all year, playing two weeks here, four weeks there, depending on the audience potential of each dinner theatre that books your show.

Dinner theatre audiences want to enjoy their evening. That means that most of the shows are shortened versions of popular comedies and farces, or stripped-down editions of musical comedies. You won't be playing Ibsen's *Hedda Gabler* on the dinner theatre circuit. And you may find you get very tired of doing Jean Kerr's *Mary, Mary* night after night. Some dinner theatres, like the Chanhassen just outside Minneapolis, produce their own shows, casting from local professionals. Others simply book packages prepared by producers in major centers such as New York and Chicago.

For beginners who need experience in performing for various kinds of audiences, dinner theatre can be a very good school. If you can handle difficult dinner customers graciously, you should be able to handle anything that might happen on the other side of the footlights.

Besides, if you are going into acting not just to gratify your own ego, but to share your talents with others, dinner theatre audiences can be as grateful as those in a conventional theatre. Of course, what is true of work possibilities for performers in commercial and nonprofit theatre also applies to the other arts and crafts of the theatre. Directors, designers, lighting technicians, costumers, carpenters, press agents—are all needed to make a theatre function effectively.

Related to dinner theatre productions are the lavish spectacles that are staged at resort hotels and in the casinos of Reno, Lake Tahoe, Las Vegas, and Atlantic City. These are eminently commercial and pay both artistic and technical staffs quite well. Little use is made of acting talents, but skills such as singing and dancing and projecting a vibrant personality can be well rewarded.

Of course, there are also commercial professional opportunities for performers and technicians in cabarets and nightclubs. Serious drama is not what is wanted, usually. Actors and actresses who are able to dance and sing with charm and who can perform comic sketches effectively can make careers out of such work.

For professionals who want to work on a television series during the fall-winter-spring season and do something in living theatre during the summer, summer stock may be the right answer, especially if you have a lot of fans who see you frequently on the TV screen. Well-known personalities from television—whether they are on a soap opera or a talk show—are frequently begged to star in summer theatre programs by commercial producers. Often it is the TV personality who "sells" the show to the audience, rather than the play that is being staged. Some summer theatres, like dinner theatres, produce their own shows. Others may form a group of summer theatres, each one packaging a show that will play at all the group's theatres. And some summer playhouses simply book shows produced for profit by independent managements. As in the other forms of commercial professional theatre, there are a variety of jobs for nonperformers, too.

Summer theatre is necessarily seasonal work. It is, however, a good place for young people to apprentice, whether as actors, dancers, singers, technical workers, or management personnel. Some colleges give credit for such internships, and some summer theatres make a point of offering special classes in the arts and crafts of theatre to their young co-workers.

Thanks to the ingenuity of Walt Disney and his staff in the way they conceived, designed, and programmed Disneyland and, later, Disney World, "theme parks" have become popular all over the U.S. The Marriott hotel interests have created the Great Adventure parks. Busch Gardens and similar theme parks have inspired many imitators. Although these may seem a novelty, they are really nothing new in America or Europe. In your grandfather's day, most American cities had what was often called a "Luna Park" outside town. New York City had Coney island amusement park and Palisades Park across the Hudson River in New Jersey. Denver had—and still has—Elitch Gardens, now over a hundred years old. Ferris wheels, roller coasters, and other exciting "rides" were a main attraction at such parks. But so were shooting galleries and other games of skill and chance, as well as snack bars and restaurants. Within such parks, usually landscaped attractively, were ornamental gardens, frequently with open-air theatres. Often, there were indoor theatres as well.

Open-air plays, concerts, and dance programs were often free to the public, the performers and technicians being paid by the park management to provide entertainment to those who had bought admission to the park itself. Indoor theatres usually charged an extra admission fee. Today, every summer in Copenhagen's Tivoli Gardens—founded in 1843—this still goes on, and it's not unusual to find American performers as the feature attractions. Back home in the U.S., however, the same phenomenon can be seen. The Disney and Marriott managements prefer young talent for their shows, so these theme park jobs are good for gaining experience. College drama credit can sometimes be arranged. Some of them do not pay much—or at all—though. This is certainly commercial theatre, even if it seems to be free. The production costs have been incorporated into the cost of the general admission to the park. In fact, the so-called free shows are one of the magnets to draw the public inside.

There is another large—and steadily growing—category in the professional theatre. This is the nonprofit theatre, sometimes called "not-for-profit" theatre. Most of these theatres are organized and financed in such a way that the artistic, technical, and management staffs are all paid fair professional wages. But they are not "commercial" in the sense that the Broadway theatre or the "road" is. Few of these theatres could make a profit even if they tried hard to do so. If one does show a profit, that money must be plowed right back into the production program to support a play or a project that is going to lose money.

This may seem a bit crazy to you. Granted, you have to be a little crazy to give up the security of a 9-to-5 job typing for Prudential Insurance to be a set designer, a stage director, or an actress. Especially when you won't be working regularly and will often be job-hunting. When that happens, not only your family will think theatre is a crazy kind of career. You may, as well.

"But," you may well ask, "who would be so crazy as to open a theatre that isn't *supposed* to make a profit? Not even to *try* to make one? Isn't that stupid?"

Actually, it's not stupid at all. It is another way of making live professional theater possible in America. It is well known in Europe, especially in Germany and Scandinavia, where there are scores of such theatres, all subsidized by states or cities that want to provide their citizens with the best that can be created in theatre art. In many of these tax-supported theatres, income from box-office or subscription ticket sales covers as little as 20 percent of the expenses of running the theatre—including salaries.

In America, the system is not yet as fully developed or as heavily subsidized as it is in Europe. But around the United States today there are over forty regional not-for-profit theatres. They are called LORT theatres—League of Resident Theatres—because of the special contract they have with Actors' Equity Association. Few of them have generous subsidies from the cities or states where they are located, but often state arts councils do give annual grants of money. The National Endowment for the Arts (NEA) also gives subsidies to selected regional resident theatres, as do private foundations such as the Rockefeller, the Ford, and others. Sometimes these grants are "Challenge Grants," which must be matched by an equal sum donated by local citizens.

In a well-managed LORT theatre, subsidies, donations, ticket sales, scholarships, and even income from snack bars and bookstalls are pooled to pay salaries, buy production materials, pay utility and maintenance bills, and provide for publicity and similar expenses. If there is a deficit at the end of the season, the theatre has a fund-raising drive to pay it off—before beginning another drive to raise money for the next season. That doesn't mean that the actors and the staff do not get paid. They do—and on time.

What it does mean, however, is that, unlike such theatres in Europe—where actors are paid on an annual basis, with a month or two-month *paid* summer vacation and a state pension plan—most American regional theatres cannot afford to have a regularly employed company, or ensemble, of performers. Usually, actors are "jobbed in" for each show in the theatre's season series, which may be four to ten productions. Some theatres do have a "core" of talented actors from which they frequently cast major roles. A few, such as William Ball's highly praised San Francisco ensemble, the American Conservatory Theatre, or A.C.T., do have a regular company of actors. What's more, the A.C.T. also has its own theatre school, in which its professional actors and technicians teach. Talented students are allowed to appear in major productions as well.

Although these regional theatres are occasionally referred to as repertory theatres—which means that several productions are played in nightly rotation, rather than one play week after week—few can actually afford the constant changes of settings. Few have enough backstage space to store all the sets and costumes needed for three rotating shows. The A.C.T., however, does manage to play repertory, as does the Yale Repertory, on occasion. When Ball first brought the A.C.T. to San Francisco from the East, his company was performing in two theatres with a large repertory. In the closing week of the season, given eight performance slots in each theatre, the company performed sixteen different plays—to prove they could do it. They have never repeated this stunt. But European theatres could. In Munich or Vienna, for instance, the state operas have at least sixty different productions stored, ready for performance. All the managements have to do is find the singers to fill the various roles on a given night.

Some performers, designers, and technicians don't like to leave theatre or film/TV producing centers such as New York and Los Angeles, fearing they might miss a chance at a good job. Others, however, welcome a five- or six-week engagement in Louisville, Seattle, Denver, Dallas, or Milwaukee. The pay is union scale. The performance challenge is professional. If it's a new play, it might even be brought to Broadway or sold to Hollywood, and the performer might go with it. Leaving New York for a whole season to work in San Francisco with the A.C.T. is a much more important decision to make. Once you have signed the contract for the season, you are obligated to honor it even if a wonderful Broadway role suddenly is offered you. Sometimes, an adjustment can be made, but it's not fair to the theatre management, the rest of the company, or the public if a season of plays has been announced with you cast in important parts, and you try to back out of the commitment.

There is another category of nonprofit theatre that pays everyone who works in it very well indeed. This is the "industrial" show. General Motors, to launch a new model of car; General Foods, to boost sales of breakfast cereals; Sears, to inspire its salesmen to move more goods. These and other major American corporations and industries often spend a lot of money on handsomely designed, cleverly written, and energetically performed shows. They help to sell their products, improve their images, or explain their policies. Whenever there is a World's Fair or International Exposition, skilled theatre artists and technicians are in great demand to create such shows for the public. In recent years, however, robots, film-loops, and videotapes have been threatening the actors' supremacy. Automated shows present few union problems, and robots don't tire the way humans do. You may never have seen one of these industrial shows. If not, that is because so many of them are not shown to the public at all, but are played for salesmen, officials, or important customers of the company that has paid for the show.

Just as seasonal as the commercial summer stock theatres is a different class of summer theatre. This is the not-for-profit outdoor drama. These shows are presented in outdoor amphitheatres during the summer in many parts of the United States, notably in the Southeastern states. There are three main kinds of outdoor drama. Perhaps best known are the Shakespeare festivals, featuring the tragedies, histories, and comedies of William Shakespeare. One of the finest of these is in Ashland, Oregon, where the season, by careful management, often finishes with a small profit rather than a loss. This profit is quickly reinvested in the following season. (Recently, the Oregon Shakespearean Festival, as this venture is called, began year-round operation with steady employment for a core of actors, staff, and administrative personnel.) The appeal of Shakespeare to the American public—at least in the summer—is so great that there are now over thirty Shakespeare festivals in the U.S., though not all of them are staged outdoors or in summer.

A second large segment of the outdoor drama activity is what is called historical drama. Among the most noted of these is Paul Green's *The Lost Colony,* staged each summer on Roanoke Island, on the Virginia coast, where Sir Walter Raleigh's first English colony in America was founded—and destroyed. Also popular are *Horn in the West,* in Boone, North Carolina; *The Hatfields and the McCoys,* in Beckley, West Virginia; and *The Stephen Foster Story,* in Bardstown, Kentucky. Historical fact and local legend are mixed by professional playwrights such as Kermit Hunter and Paul Green, who won a Pulitzer Prize for drama. Professional actors are often engaged for major roles; technicians and managers are also employed on a professional basis. Many of these large-scale outdoor shows, because of the size of the casts and the spectacular nature of some special effects, cannot afford to pay everyone, or even very much to those they do pay. Such things vary from show to show, so any young theatre worker who wants to work in this area of summer production would be well advised to find out just what he can expect in terms of work and pay.

Along with Shakespeare and history, there are also some open-air Passion plays and religious dramas. The one in Spearfish, South Dakota, was inspired by the famous Oberammergau Passion Play. It was created in the U.S. by artists from Germany who had fled Hitler and the Nazis. There are also several outdoor summer musical comedy theatres. New York City has one at Jones Beach, for years under the guidance of the late orchestra leader Guy Lombardo.

Almost all of these theatre operations are provided for the summer enjoyment of local citizens and of tourists. Studies have shown that thousands, even millions, of dollars are spent each season in the communities that sponsor such shows. Even if a festival or a pageant loses money because its production costs are greater than the income from sold-out houses, communities consider that subsidizing the deficit is a good investment. What they pay out to balance the production books, they more than make back at the cash registers of hotels, motels, restaurants, gas stations, boutiques, and antique shops. That's just fine for the community economically. It pleases the tourists, who not only get to see the U.S. but also may learn some history in an exciting way or come to appreciate Shakespeare's genius more deeply. Best of all for theatre people, these productions provide paid jobs. For those who are just beginning as professionals, there are few playwrights as challenging as Shakespeare. And there are few performance experiences more demanding than working in a history drama outdoors on a huge stage with a huge cast and live horses!

WORKING IN THE THEATRE

The idea of being a featured performer may be exciting and glamorous to you. The truth is that for every star or featured artist there are hundreds of actors, singers, dancers, and musicians who are seldom or never the center of audience attention. But that doesn't mean that their own contribution isn't important to the total effect of a play, revue, or musical comedy in production. Without the supporting performers, where would the star be? In any case, the concept of the star is primarily a commercial one. It is discouraged in nonprofit theatres and experimental, "alternative" projects. Increasingly, the concept of the ensemble as a skilled, experienced, interrelating group of performers is being stressed.

Another truth, and an unpleasant one, is that hundreds, even thousands of performers cannot find regular work in theatre, cinema, or radio/television broadcasting. Every year, more hundreds of high school and college graduates stream into New York City and Los Angeles, convinced that they will find a place for themselves in some part of the performing arts. To be realistic, however, it is just not possible, given the potential job market, for all of these newcomers to find employment—especially since they will have to compete with all the others who came before them.

That doesn't mean that someone with talent, training, and a driving ambition won't make his or her way to the top. It happens all the time. In the theatre, the climb up the ladder to artistic recognition and public affection tends to be slower than it is in films or television. So if you think you have what it takes to be a successful performer, why not try? If you are easily discouraged, that's fine, too. You will probably save yourself heartbreak later on.

Of course, if you are determined to work in the theatre, really *work,* and earn a fairly regular living, your chances will be much better if you prepare yourself for a career in technical theatre or in performing arts management. Although many theatres—dinner theatres, resident theatres, and, of course, Broadway theatres—do not have ongoing jobs for actors and other performers, they do have positions for business managers, press representatives, box-office managers, subscription sales personnel, carpenters, lighting technicians, stagehands, wardrobe mistresses, and other trained people who help support the theatre's production program. It might not seem at all glamorous to be down in the theatre basement washing sweaty leotards or out in the scene shop scrubbing paint off some flats. In fact, it isn't glamorous at all. But it can, in a real sense, be exciting; you are part of the living theatre. Part of a new production being rushed toward opening night—and, at the same time, part of a tradition that goes back to the Greeks and beyond, into our forgotten past on this earth.

There will always be the possibility of rivalries, fights, and disappointments when you work in the theatre. There's good reason for describing some theatre people as having an "artistic temperament." Sometimes jealousy or a temper flare-up can be sparked by a director's giving an important role to one actress and not casting another at all, even in a small part. This is perfectly understandable. At other times, a performer who is hard to get along with on stage and off may be suffering from a real sense of inadequacy, of insecurity. Some people try to cover their own shortcomings by ignoring them, by shows of temper, or by blaming other performers for their own mistakes. At the end of a successful run of a commercial show, with no further acting jobs in sight, a performer may justifiably be worried. But seasoned, talented, well-trained performers take all the upsets of their profession in stride. They don't want to ruffle their fellow players or spoil the production with their own problems.

Generally, even in a commercial production, after which the cast may never work together again, there is a spirit of cooperation, of mutual pride in what is being done. This is especially so in those institutional theatres that can afford to pay a regular ensemble. In such situations, players work with each other almost every day in rehearsal and performance. A sensitivity to each other's moods and attitudes develops, a receptivity that can help create very truthful, compelling work on stage. It also encourages a friendly, supportive atmosphere off stage, in rehearsal and in life outside the theatre.

Since America does not yet have a network of subsidized national theatres and is not likely to set up such a system in the near future, work opportunities—especially on an annual basis, as is standard in many European theatres—will remain limited. Despite that, there are still a number of large American cities that have no resident professional theatre, though they have potential audiences of thousands. There are also quite a few smaller cities which, because they have several colleges and industrial complexes nearby, have a considerable group of educated people who could support a professional theatre if someone were to create it for them. Nor is theatre only for college graduates; it speaks to everyone.

What this means to the young would-be performer, playwright, director, designer, manager, or technical expert is that you can—if you have the courage and a sound plan—form your own not-for-profit theatre. In school, it might be a good idea to start discussing such a move. If you are a leader, or even a good committee member, draw together fellow students in the various arts and crafts of theatre. You may be able to find all the talents and skills you will need in your own school, or supplement them with established professionals. This takes a lot of hard thought and planning, of course.

It is worth a lot to be able to work with congenial and capable artists and technicians who are also friends. It is also a good idea to have a second job possibility: a teaching credential, secretarial skills, membership in a craft union. When you find a city that seems right for the theatre you want to develop, all of you will probably have to earn your living, at least for a while, at other jobs. This can have a valuable side effect on establishing your ensemble in the community. If you live and work there and, say, make real professional theatre only on weekends at first, you may win your neighbors' support much more rapidly. If you come into town like a bunch of carefree kids, expecting everyone to love you and help you, you may be ignored or actively discouraged. You may be thought of as "outsiders."

This is the way William Ball started his A.C.T., which is now the pride of San Francisco. Ellis Rabb and Rosemary Harris did the same with a group of friends—all capable performers—when they formed the Association of Producing Artists (APA). The APA eventually spent its performance seasons with major work in Ann Arbor, Michigan, and in New York City, on Broadway, after awkward beginnings. It also toured successful productions around the country. Unfortunately, because of funding and management problems, it ceased to exist. While it was alive, however, it gave a number of America's best-known performers their first chance to show the public their talents. It gave them the opportunity to gain experience in both classics and commercial comedies.

When the remarkably talented and well-trained first class graduated from the newly formed Drama Division of the Juilliard School in New York, John Houseman, the famed director/producer/actor and head of drama, set up The Acting Company for them. He realized how few jobs were open, no matter how talented his graduates. Today, this fine troupe takes in young performers, through auditions, from good drama schools all over the country. Playing a repertory of interesting contemporary and classic dramas, the company spends most of its year on tour, sharing the pleasure of live theatre with audiences in many American communities that otherwise would have little or no professional performance.

Now let's look at some of the specific possibilities for careers in the theatre. Remember that some of these have their counterparts in other performance media, such as films and broadcasting. You may, as an actor, find more work in television than in theatre, for instance.

Be sure to study the job descriptions in the other sections of this book as well. This section is concerned only with those jobs that are directly involved in theatre production, such as the performers, directors, producers, and designers. All those valuable people who make it possible for a theatre production or organization to operate, to find its audiences, are discussed under technical theatre and performing arts management. They are essential to the success of the theatre—even if that means only breaking even at the end of a run or a season.

Playwright

If writing a play is all it takes to be a playwright, then America is full of playwrights. Getting your play produced is quite a different matter. Not to mention making some money from it. And making a full-time living as a playwright is most difficult of all. But without new playwrights with new ideas, new characters, new tales to tell on stage, our theatre would not renew itself. Without the play, there is nothing for the other creative theatre people to work on. How can they show their talents if they have no vehicle?

The American theatre is, in fact, so hungry for *good* new plays that there are a number of play contests, playwrights' scholarships, subsidized theatre writing programs, script workshops, and tryout centers all set up to encourage the development of plays and writers. That means that if you show signs of talent as a playwright, even in high school, you may have a much easier time of it than a classmate who wants to act. Play publishers, national theatre organizations, even community theatres sponsor playwriting contests. Winning one of these may not win you a scholarship to the Yale School of Drama or the California Institute of the Arts. But it will bring your work to the attention of theatre professionals and drama teachers. That could lead to professional production or to a college scholarship for further study.

Owning a typewriter and knowing how to type isn't enough. You need to be a careful observer of nature and the life around you. You need to be able to be detached from it at times; at other times, very close, very responsive, very sympathetic to it. But writing a play doesn't mean that you put down on the page everything you see and hear. You have to select. Often, you have to rearrange or improvise new images and actions based on what you have already experienced. Imagination and fantasy are valuable aids to the young writer. In our 20th-century theatre, the emphasis, thanks to the works of Ibsen and Chekhov, has long been on realism. But some of the best contemporary dramas are plays of pure imagination, based on some human truth.

A number of books are available on play analysis and playwriting, some of which are listed in the Appendix. Some writers, however, insist that there are no such things as *rules.* Or, at least, that you cannot learn how to write a good play just by reading a book. That last statement is probably true. But you can learn a lot about structure—how to organize your plot, to motivate your characters, to phrase your dialogue so that the play will *work* on stage both for the performers who have to give it life and for the audience who want to enjoy it. A very good way to begin is by reading a lot of plays, classic and modern. Read Shakespeare, the Greeks. Read Neil Simon's comedies. Read Samuel Beckett's *Waiting for Godot.* As you read, ask yourself what the playwright intends; what does he want the play to say, to do for an audience? How does he make it possible for the performers to achieve that? What does he want his audience to do: think? laugh? cry? get angry? If you get used to analyzing plays to see how they are put together—don't read them just for enjoyment—you will be learning a lot about how to write a play.

In English and language classes, where plays are often studied, is a good place to begin. You can ask your instructor to help you. Chances are that, if he or she knows you are really interested in writing plays, the classwork may be redirected for you and the other students to give you a taste of playwriting. You can learn from reading novels and short stories as well; they are often adapted for the stage, cinema, and television. Don't just read. *See* plays as often as you can. Even the most amateurish production can be useful; it can show you vividly the play's strengths and weaknesses.

It's important not just to be a reader/writer. You shouldn't try to write professionally for the stage until you have some training in actual performance and production. When you have been in some plays, you will better appreciate what an actor does, how he may work to make your creations come alive. At the typewriter, you may think some dialogue sounds wonderful. But try it out loud—it may be awful: difficult to pronounce, awkwardly expressed, unnatural. If you know something about stage design, set construction, costume building, lighting possibilities, different kinds of stages, you won't ask a theatre company to build you 100 costumes, 40 sets, and provide a revolving stage where one does not exist. Working in the practical theatre can help make you a very practical—but no less inspired—playwright.

Few high schools have much in the way of special instruction for would-be playwrights. Many colleges, however, have courses and entire programs at the undergraduate and graduate levels. As a potential or practical writer for the theatre, your two best textbooks, however, are *life* and the *theatre*. While still in school, though, you will discover that courses in psychology, sociology, history, art, music, and languages can be very useful parallel studies with theatre and English classes.

A major, successful Broadway production can earn you a lot of money. You will be paid a royalty every time the show is performed. If there is a national tour, a Chicago company, a London company—all these performances will pay you royalties. You receive a royalty every time an American regional theatre or a German state-subsidized theatre does your play. Every performance by a community theatre or a college or high school group earns you a royalty—unless the group fails to get permission from your publisher and does the drama illegally. Even plays that have failed on Broadway—such as John Patrick's *Everybody Loves Opal,* which closed almost immediately to negative reviews—have gone on to be real annuities for their authors, thanks to school and community productions.

Having had a success—or even a failure—on Broadway doesn't guarantee that your next play will be optioned for production. Some well-known playwrights have several unproduced plays in their desks. Steadily rising production costs, producers' inability to get the right elements—players, director, designers—together, changing public tastes, nonavailability of a Broadway theatre: these are all factors that may condemn a perfectly good play to lose a large-scale commercial production.

Often, when this happens, the writer may offer his play to an Off-

Off Broadway showcase theatre or have it done at a playwrights' conference such as the O'Neill Center in Waterford, Connecticut. Such previews are often preludes to Broadway versions. Regional theatres are eager to have at least one new play, one premiere, in their seasonal program, so that is another possibility for production. And important regional productions do reach Broadway. Michael Cristofer's *Shadow Box,* which won a Pulitzer Prize, bowed on Broadway after workshop production at Los Angeles' Mark Taper Forum and professional staging at New Haven's resident theatre, the Long Wharf.

Artistic recognition in the theatre can lead to lucrative work writing for films and television as well. You will customarily collect royalties on plays you write whenever there is a performance or when someone buys a copy of the play, but you can also be paid a fee for writing. You can even be commissioned to write a drama; the commission fee may be treated as an advance payment against future production royalties. If you don't already write for films, your play may still be bought by a film producer—for a good sum, if you have a good agent to represent you—who will have someone else turn it into a shooting script. You might even be well paid for the right to use characters you have created in a film or TV series written by another author. Or you can become wealthy working as a cinema/TV writer yourself.

You may have to have a regular job—possibly as a typist or an editor—to permit you to continue writing in your spare time. Few would-be playwrights actually achieve success, especially continuing success. It's true that Neil Simon is the wealthiest playwright who has ever lived. It's also true that there are thousands of Simon imitators who will never make a penny as playwrights. Be wary of fame and prepared for disappointment.

If you want a regular job as a playwright, you might be lucky enough—if you have shown talent and had some early success—to be hired as a playwright-in-residence or a dramaturg in an institutional theatre. Usually, residencies are only for a season, to help a writer finish a new play and give it some workshop exposure. A dramaturg, who helps the artistic director of such a theatre plan the season's program by selecting classics, reading new scripts, and even contributing his own work, can stay several years at one theatre.

Joining the Dramatists Guild is one useful and pleasant compensation for becoming a recognized, produced playwright. The Guild is of professional assistance to you, and it also helps you to get to know other practicing playwrights. Once you are really working in the theatre as a playwright, you will be amazed at how easy it is to get to know most of the noted actors, directors, and designers you have long admired from a distance. For all its occasional phoniness, heartbreak, hysteria, and "hype," the theatre is in many ways a "family."

Writing the play, of course, poses problems. But those aren't the only ones. Getting your play *read* and then *produced* are what finally count. You could begin writing, if you were another Neil Simon, by working with your older brother on TV scripts for major network comedies series. But that route is open to few. Or you could start out like Edward Albee, who lived in a cheap room on New York's West Side and worked as a Western Union messenger while he was finding himself as a young playwright. His play *Zoo Story* has echoes of this experience in it. You don't have to leave home and rush off to New York or Los Angeles in order to write plays. If you want to get them seen, however, you need to be resourceful: win a contest, get a scholarship, find an agent who believes in you, have a professional regional production.

It's an uphill road, of course. But what kind of reward or recognition could you expect if you never made the climb? Remember, no one owes you a living as a playwright. No one *has* to produce your play. No one has a *duty* to buy a ticket to see it. You have to make all of those things happen because you are a talented professional, full of creative imagination.

Commercial Producer

Unlike the artistic director or the business manager of a regional resident theatre or other nonprofit drama group, the commercial producer has no guaranteed, contractual, salaried position in a clearly defined organizational structure. His risks are high, so he has to be something of a gambler. Theatre isn't quite like roulette, however, so he also has to know a lot about contemporary theatre, its working talents, its problems, its audience tastes, its critics, its financial difficulties. As one experienced Broadway producer says, "If you knew what I know about the state of the theatre today, you'd *never* produce a play!" But that doesn't stop him from continually taking risks on plays and performers he believes in. Fortunately, his theatre knowledge and his gambler's instincts prove him right more often than he is wrong.

The producer's foremost responsibility, once he has found a play he likes and has paid the playwright for an option to produce it, is to raise the money necessary to produce it. If he can't manage to do this, when the option lapses some other producer can then option the play. Maurice Valency once made quite a bit of money out of repeated options on a play he wrote, *The Thracian Horses.* When it was finally produced, critics found it a disappointment.

In the days of David Belasco and Charles and Daniel Frohman, major producers either owned or controlled theatres, in which they produced the plays they liked, in the way they liked, with the performers they favored. Their tastes and styles were well known and approved by the public. They could afford to invest their own money. They then retained control of all aspects of production, and they prospered. When the Shubert brothers had taken ownership or control of most New York theatres and a large number around the U.S. they too became active producers, to fill their houses and those of their clients with popular shows. At one time they had no less than fourteen separate companies of the musical *Blossom Time* on the road.

There are still some producers who invest their own money in commercial productions. Either they inherited wealth, or they have made a lot of money. Some have made it in the theatre; others, like Roger Stevens, who once owned the Empire State Building, in real estate. With the tremendous risks facing a new production today, however, it is unwise for any producer to be the sole investor. A major musical can cost $1.5 million. A major musical can also close after its opening night on Broadway. In the 1978–79 season, one of them did just that. Curiously, it was called *A Broadway Musical.* If a rich man needs a tax loss, Broadway investing is a good place to find one.

Because of the way Broadway shows are regulated in their financing, structure, and operation, a producer can still make a nice profit for his efforts and skills used in bringing together a group of investors, or "angels," to provide the necessary money, and in engaging good performers, designers, and a talented director. Of course, he has to have chosen a good script to begin with. But if all the elements come together artistically, he may well have both a critical and a popular success on Broadway. There are other profits to be made from subsequent productions and subsidiary rights, depending on what arrangements he had made with the playwright and his investors. His success also breeds confidence. He will find himself swamped with new playwrights' dramas as well as plays by famous or forgotten authors. Directors, stars, young hopefuls, would-be investors: all want to work with him.

What this means to you is that you do not have to be related to a Rockefeller or a Mellon in order to become a commercial producer. You don't have to inherit a million; you don't even have to earn a million before you begin. It is true that a lot of new producers are wealthy people—often young people—but many of these bring to production only their money. They have no knowledge of the theatre, especially the financial, management side of it. Lacking that expertise is dangerous. It's a good way to make bad choices, be cheated, and even humiliated. In the theatre, ignorance is *not* bliss.

Some of New York's most interesting, adventurous producers are young people who bring, not a fortune, but a lot of knowledge about theatre practice and intelligent taste to their jobs. Producing is not for those who hate math. It's not for those with weak nerves and no patience. It's not for those who lack the imagination to envision various possibilities. It's not for those who cannot analyze problems or synthesize solutions. It's not for those who are awkward or shy around others. It's not for professional pessimists.

It makes absolutely no sense to plan to become a producer on leaving school. You probably couldn't get started anyway, without the experience and confidence it takes to option a good play and get wealthy people to lend you their money. But if the idea appeals to you and you think you have the habits of mind that could suit you to such work, there are a number of things you can do to prepare yourself for the day when you really could try your hand at commercial production. And, if you get cold feet about the risk-taking necessary for Broadway and similar commercial ventures, you will still be very well equipped to work in the nonprofit theatre.

High school is not too early a time to concentrate on math studies, any business-training courses—including typing and shorthand—that are available, and social studies that will help you better understand how to get along with others from diverse backgrounds. You should also take any drama or theatre-practice courses that are offered, to start learning the "nuts and bolts" of performance and production. If there are none, then get involved in school and community plays. At the college level, there are customarily many more courses, both in theatre and in the studies needed in management. Psychology, economics, and business administration are obvious choices.

As has been said, there are always thousands of young people who dream of sudden fame from an acting career. There is no shortage of actors. But, as with talented playwrights, the theatre really needs brilliant young producers and other management people. Fortunately, performing arts management courses are now being developed at a number of colleges. In New York City, at Brooklyn College, an MFA is offered in this area of expertise. Such studies, with attendant practical internships in New York theatres, are good preparation for commercial producers.

These are not the only routes to becoming a producer, however.

Sometimes wealthy playwrights or directors, in despair of getting a play produced, do it themselves, with their own or other people's money. If they have learned enough about the theatre and the all-too-fickle audience, their instincts may be right. They may have a real hit. But if their motives were only to feed their egos, they may lose everything. Training in law, accounting, or stage management can also be a useful foundation for becoming a producer. Harold Prince and his first producing partner, Robert Griffith, began as stage managers on the musical comedy *Wonderful Town.* Working as an assistant producer is also an excellent way to learn the ropes.

Producers must of course be effective businessmen, but they also have to be *showmen.* That calls for a certain flamboyance. At the same time, they need to be cautious and constant students of human nature, not only to cope with artistic temperaments, but also to keep from being cheated or deceived by colleagues. Theatre may indeed be a big family, but what family doesn't have its liars and swindlers? If your cousin the theatre owner gives you a contract to sign, be *sure* to read the fine print. Mistakes caused by misreading the motives and intentions of others can cause immense losses.

There is big money to be made in commercial production. And producing experience in the theatre can be carried over into film and TV production, though there are some important differences.

Finding a script, raising the money, and engaging a director and performers are not by any means the end of a producer's work. He has to find the right theatre and make a good deal for using it. He has to get the sets and costumes built as handsomely but as reasonably as possible. He has to oversee publicity and sales campaigns. With his assistant or assistants, he supervises or monitors every aspect of production preparation, including the direction.

Stage Director

Angry actors, smarting from criticisms—often constructive ones—given them in their "notes" after rehearsal by a director, have been heard to refer to all directors as failed actors. That is certainly not true of America's most talented stage directors. Most of them have, of course, studied acting, read all the theatre works of Konstantin Stanislavski, investigated the techniques of Grotowski and Chaikin, and even spent some time with Lee Strasberg at the Actors Studio. A good director has to know how actors feel. He should also know how they can work. Different performers have different methods. Different roles often call for different approaches.

When an actor runs out of methods, of ideas, of images, of instincts—even of energy, the director has to be ready to stimulate him. The director has to find other ways of helping the actor to master his role, to make it a part of himself. If the director is basically a frustrated actor at heart, he may be giving a performance for his cast instead of really rehearsing the play. Or he may be forcing some of the actors to play their parts the way he would play them if he had the talent and the chance to do so. It's one thing to have studied acting, realizing that it was not where your talent really lay. It is quite another thing to have given up acting—by popular demand, perhaps—when it was *all* that you wanted to do in the theatre. If the latter happens, such a person will not make a good director. Some successful actors, of course, have also proved excellent directors. Anthony Quayle is one, though he tends to concentrate his greatest attention on the actor who is playing the role he himself might have played. Sir Laurence Olivier has often avoided that problem by both directing and playing the leading role, using a stand-in for those moments when he felt he needed to see the shape of the play from the director's seat in the auditorium.

In the commercial theatre, the director is most often engaged by the producer. Sometimes, however, a director will bring a good new play to a producer and ask him to finance a production. Because the producer has so much responsibility in a commercial production, the director's choices and authority may at times be somewhat limited. In the nonprofit theatre, on the other hand, the director might well have no—or very few—problems with interference with his decisions about casting, set and costume designs, and similar artistic matters. This is especially true if he is also the artistic director of such a theatre.

Notable works of art are seldom created by committees, even in the theatre. So somebody finally has to be the boss when it comes to questions of taste, emphasis, style, and interpretation. That person should be the director, not the producer. If the producer has chosen well, he won't feel the need to interfere. Really good directors, frustrated by meddling, insecure producers, are apt to quit.

But this means that the director must not only have a lot of self-confidence in his artistic talent, but also be able to stand up to a tough producer or a troublesome performer and resolve the problems without destroying the person or the production. That's not easy. You can learn a lot about dealing with others from psychology and sociology courses—not to mention speech classes in discussion and persuasion. But you won't develop the ability to get along with people when you are in charge just from reading a textbook.

Nor will you be a good director just because you get A's in English for your essays on Shakespeare's plays. You may be very good at analyzing a play's structure, at understanding what it is trying to say to the audience, at knowing how the characters can be cast and interpreted, but you still may lack the skills of being able to explain that to other artists and get them to bring such understanding to life on stage. If you cannot communicate your own ideas about the play, or get your fellow artists to develop theirs for you, your staging will probably be a disaster.

If you are very good at getting along with others, that is still of no great value if you don't have some understanding of the play and how to make it work on stage. You do not have to be a "leader of men" in order to direct. Some very calm, quiet men and women are among our best directors today. Their authority over the production and the cast comes from their undeniable talent, their insight, their experience, and often from their thoughtfulness of co-workers. They do not rant and rage to make the actors, designers, and technicians live in fear of them—though an occasional burst of anger when someone is habitually late or inadequate may help clear the air.

Intelligence, insight, experience, confidence, kindness: all are excellent qualities in a director. Some directors, it's true, get by through copying other people's productions of the same show, or imitating old ideas and styles in a new production. These people are not creative, and both critics and public are aware of it. Those who play the tyrant don't often have long careers, unless they have most of the good qualities as well.

Aside from school studies in literature, theatre, and psychology, a would-be director also can never read enough plays on his own. He should go to the theatre often, to see new plays, to see how other directors work, and to become acquainted with new performing and design talents.

A good director is usually in demand, if not in the commercial theatre—where the number of productions is limited by financing and available theatres—then in regional and college theatre. Some stage directors work equally well in film and television, although the nature of those two media is somewhat different in the demands they make on directorial skills. Expecially commercials. Directors don't often get rich from the legitimate theatre, but they can command big fees in filmmaking.

In theatre, as in clothing, there are fads and fashions. Some fine directors—not to mention performers and designers—may be the rage for several seasons and then be forgotten by the commercial stage. When this happens, the director may decide, if he can, to work entirely in television. Or he may create his own showcase theatre or accept the artistic directorship of a regional resident theatre. Occasionally, he decides to give up the struggle for survival in the marketplace and retreat to the tenured safety and deceptive tranquility of a college drama department. Now, or someday soon, you may find yourself studying with someone who has already had his or her successes on Broadway. Or you may have a young instructor who is getting up the courage to quit teaching and try the professional theatre.

To work professionally as a director, you have to belong to certain unions, such as Actors' Equity Association, the Directors Guild of America, Inc., or the Society of Stage Directors and Choreographers. But first you have to get started. Your work has to be seen and reviewed. You can gain experience directing school and community productions, but these are seldom seen by professionals. If you have directed a college show that reaches the finals of the American College Theatre Festival at the John F. Kennedy Center for the Performing Arts, in Washington, D.C., there is a good chance that it will be reviewed by influential East Coast critics and seen by some agents and producers, who are always on the lookout for new talent. As with producers, being a director's assistant is good training and a possible opening into professional work.

If you live near a regional theatre and you are able to convince the artistic director of your ability, you might be allowed to direct a workshop or studio production. Resident theatres such as the Guthrie, in Minneapolis; the Seattle Rep, in Seattle; or the Alley, in Houston, are regularly reviewed by local critics whose reviews appear in leading newspapers. These, if the play or the production is notable, find their way onto the desks of New York and Los Angeles producers, agents, and critics.

A great many would-be directors work their way into the professional theatre through various forms of summer theatre. Others come to New York and try to get the chance to stage a show at one of the many OOBA theatres. That doesn't mean that you and your theatre-oriented friends couldn't set up something like a showcase theatre in your own community. You could—and there are now a lot of them in such cities as Chicago, Minneapolis, Seattle, San Francisco, and Los Angeles. That there aren't more of these around the country is the fault of the young talent that deserts its own native grounds in favor of New York.

Gordon Davidson, of the Mark Taper Forum, is an interesting example of the usual process in reverse. Davidson's father, Professor Joseph Davidson, was for many years a beloved teacher of directing at Brooklyn College in New York City. Young Davidson not only did not go to college in Brooklyn, but he also didn't start out as a theatre major. He chose engineering! When he finally did get interested in theatre—he says now that he was avoiding it earlier—he didn't go back to New York but went to Los Angeles instead to head a new, intimate experimental theatre in the lavish complex of the downtown Music Center. His work there has been highly experimental, and also successful. A number of his productions have been restaged in New York, on Broadway and Off, proving that good work cannot be kept a secret even if it is done thousands of miles from Manhattan.

Choreographer

Dances are seldom used in plays, although some form of folk or social dance may be needed to create atmosphere or heighten the seeming reality of the production. In revues, cabaret acts, historical dramas, Shakespearean productions, musical comedies, operettas, and operas, of course, dance is often an element. Musicals are usually the longest-running Broadway productions and the biggest money-makers. They are community and college production favorites. In other countries, American musicals are very popular as well. American choreographers, or dance captains from the original Broadway shows, are often invited abroad to recreate not just the dances but the entire New York production. And they are very well paid for this work.

Because dance and opera theatre has a section of its own, the description of a potential choreographer's basic qualities, necessary education, and possibilities for gaining experience will be found there.

Performers

You may wonder why this category is not titled: Actor/Actress. It could be. But the title used is more inclusive of the varied talents needed in theatre performance. Not so long ago, before television had taken away a lot of the former theatre audience, there were actors and actresses who prided themselves on being trained only to perform roles in plays. They had never studied singing and had no intention of doing so. If they could dance at all, they did the waltz, the fox-trot, or other social dances of the time. Many of them could play no musical instrument, even if the script called for them to do so. In the tragic climax of Henrik Ibsen's *Hedda Gabler,* for instance, Hedda plays the piano before she shoots herself. Fortunately the playwright lets her draw some curtains so the audience doesn't have to see either of these shocking actions.

Today, with the popularity of musical comedy not only on Broadway but also on the dinner theatre circuit, actors who want to work need to be able to sing and dance with some skill. Being able to play the piano, the guitar, or some other instrument can also be very useful. Special skills such as magic and juggling are also occasionally required. Sometimes an actor may be asked to walk a tightrope. Or ride a unicycle, as Joseph Mahar did in a lively play about Northern Ireland, *Spokesong.*

History repeats itself. In the Middle Ages, after theatre had been officially suppressed for centuries, strolling players had to act, sing, dance, do acrobatics, perform magic tricks, walk the tightrope, and live on very little. Both Shakespeare's and Molière's ensembles also had to have many talents to please their audiences. In 18th-century America, the early troupers had to perform not only Shakespeare's tragedies and Sheridan's comedies, but also Mozart's operas. Programs surviving from that time also show that some of them walked the tightrope, too. Then it was called "rope dancing."

Sometimes a playwright or a director uses a trained musician or specialty artist in a production, especially if he cannot find an actor who can do what is needed. The difficulty is that, lacking acting training, the musician or the novelty performer may not be able to bring to the production the same belief in character that the rest of the cast do. If you are interested in playing a musical instrument, being expert in kung fu, developing as a dancer or singer—but also want to act on stage—you must of course master those special skills. But you must at the same time develop as an actor as well.

You will seldom be called on to use Oriental martial arts in a stage role. Still, it's nice to know you can do it if needed, or that you could teach someone else to do it. In the conservatory of San Francisco's A.C.T., actors teach each other and the younger students all kinds of skills they have learned in and out of the theatre. Virtually every form of folk and social dance, as well as classical and modern, is studied. Everyone learns to play at least one musical instrument. Stage fighting, with old and modern weapons or with bare fists, is taught. There is even a class in which actors and novices study patterns of laughter. One A.C.T. teacher says there are over eighty different kinds of laughter. Many of them can be used to good dramatic effect on stage when they grow out of thoughtful rehearsals in which they are organic to scenes in the play.

In high school and college, most young people who become interested in the theatre first think they want to be actors. Perhaps the attraction is in the fame and wealth that a number of popular young stars seem to enjoy. Possibly the motivation comes from being ashamed or embarrassed about the way they look or how other people treat them. Putting on a costume, creating an attractive makeup, and becoming someone else, often far more glamorous and interesting than you think you are, can be a means of escaping reality. This is not speculation. Some people do, in fact, become actors to have some different identity, if only for a few hours each night on stage. Famous performers have talked about the pleasure of "putting on the mask" and becoming someone else.

Still, it's difficult to be a really skilled actor—unless you operate entirely on instinct, which isn't always reliable—if you aren't aware of who you really are. If you want to hide from yourself, from self-analysis, you are not apt to be an effective performer. A good actor needs both instinct and intelligence. There are, it's true, some actors who make a decent living without ever showing much imagination or thought in their work. But they tend to be cast to type; they play what they are. Of course there are also those *personalities*—some of them very clever—who make no attempt to create a character at all. They play themselves, which is probably just what their fans want, with only a few strokes of caricature or stereotyping to suggest that the playwright intended them to be someone else we've never seen before. Such performers also do well as individual acts in clubs and cabarets. Some began as dancers, or singers, or even as stand-up comics, not as actors. But many popular comics, such as Jack Benny, George Burns, and Bob Hope, went on to act roles as well in plays and films.

If you were to add up the possible rewards in an acting career, in honesty, you'd have to put fame and wealth near the bottom for most people who try it. But acting is a way to create a work of art, an *interpretation* of a role only partly sketched in by the playwright. It is a way to share your abilities, to give pleasure to others. It is a way to win appreciation, especially valuable if you think you couldn't do that in an ordinary job. Even if you don't make a lot of money, admiring reviews from respected critics and letters from spectators who have enjoyed your work are both tangible and spiritual rewards. Some people go into the theatre to find anonymity behind the actor's mask, as noted, but a lot more take up acting in hopes that they will be recognized, not only in Sardi's and Chasen's, but also on the street. They don't want their lives and their names to be just statistics, when all is said and done.

Just because people tell you you are good-looking, have a nice figure or well-developed muscles, and a terrific personality, don't think those are one-way tickets to acting success. They won't hurt, but they aren't enough by themselves unless some directorial Dr. Frankenstein takes you in hand and makes you into his or her kind of performer. This happens more often in films, where skilled directors, makeup, lighting, and cameramen can create an illusion that has very little to do with what you are—or were—and what talents you might have. This kind of exploitation often will require that you change your name. How about "Marilyn Monroe"? If you know how to live with such a career—being someone else's ventriloquist's dummy—you may get rich. Otherwise, you may end in tragedy—or simply forgotten, because you never developed any real internal resources or techniques. Such performers seldom succeed on stage. Their lack of talent and training is all too nakedly exposed. They cannot believably sustain a character for two hours live.

You don't have to be pretty, sexy, tall, or blond to succeed as an actor. Woody Allen isn't tall. Karl Malden isn't pretty. Who knows who is a real blond? Sexual attractiveness is often in the spectator's eye. In an era stressing what is real, there is always work for actors who look like real people instead of Greek gods.

What you do have to have, in addition to intelligence and instinct, however, is *belief* in yourself, health, physical stamina for long hours of taxing rehearsal and performance, ability to relax in the tensest of situations, energy, emotional responsiveness, and ability to communicate and interact with others, both as fellow performers and as audiences. You need to be able to accept well-intended criticism from a director and use it to good effect. You also need to be able to screen out malicious criticism and not let it hurt or depress you. Sometimes criticism that is well-intended may hurt because you believe it is really unfair. You have to handle this.

When you are still in school, it's not too soon to study singing and dancing seriously, even taking special courses after school hours. Some acting teachers, such as John Houseman, think it's a mistake to study acting in one's early teens. You need, he says, to mature, to have some experience of life. In college, you can major in drama, but you shouldn't concentrate on acting. You need to learn something about all aspects of theatre production, to understand how it fits together. Work on music and dance should be continued; work on voice, diction, dialects, and movement should be begun. When you are working professionally, you will still need to continue classwork in some of these areas, not just to improve, but to hold your ground. The muscles and the techniques need to be exercised all the time.

Few colleges or universities, even at the graduate level, offer complete professional conservatory training. Some professional schools such as the Juilliard School's Drama Division are well regarded. The San Francisco training of the A.C.T. has been praised. But there are ups and downs in a school's quality, and students find they interact differently with some instructors than their colleagues do. One actor will swear by his favorite teacher. Another will swear *at* him: "The worst teacher I ever had!"

Possibly because so much acting is mirroring life, an actor's learning, observing, and training is always going on—if he is conscientious. This can mean that, even when you are out of work, you will spend what little money you have to rent studio space for exercises or to pay for vocal lessons. But if you are really serious about your craft, your art, you will make those sacrifices. If not, you should have taken up typing. At least you'd be more apt to find work. The reality is that most members of Actors' Equity—the union for stage actors—earn less than $3,500 a year.

Possibilities for working as an actor, fortunately, exist in several forms of theatre, already discussed, as well as in other performing arts media. What is not always possible is a living wage. Some actors go on to become directors: Austin Pendleton and Robert Moore have done that. Some become playwrights. Some give up and open a studio to train other actors. New York is full of such studios.

For actors, it's a problem not only to get noticed initially, but to keep your name, your face, your talents vividly in the minds of producers, directors, casting directors, agents, journalists, and critics—not to mention the public. Sometimes your own agent will forget all about you. Belonging to the major performance unions, such as AEA, AFTRA, SAG, and AGVA, is important. These are listed in the Appendix, with explanations of what they are and what they mean to an actor.

Actors have to have up-to-date résumés and photo-composites to leave with agents, producers, and directors when they "make the rounds." They should maintain a "book" documenting their past work for those who want more detail. Interviews, auditions, screen tests: all are methods of showing a performer's abilities, but the process has to be repeated over and over, for each new job possibility. Even a showcase production at an OOBA theatre can involve five or six weeks of hard work with no guarantee that any producer, director, agent, or critic will come to see the show.

No wonder an actor breathes a sigh of relief when he or she lands an important role in a TV sitcom or soap opera! Unfortunately, such work can also "type" you with the public so that they no longer want to see you being somebody other than your TV-self. If the show is canceled or your role is eliminated, you may find yourself out of work for some time. So an actor's life is not necessarily a happy or a prosperous one. Even for the most successful of performers, there are tremendous ups and downs. But if you are determined to try, you might as well. If you don't, you will probably never forgive yourself. If you make the effort in the right way when you are young, and you fail, or feel you aren't going to be as good as you'd like to be, it's better to find that out early. You can then prepare for a different career. Perhaps as a performing arts manager?

Designers

There was a time when a theatre manager could order a "deluxe parlor setting" from a company in Chicago for as little as $350—but that was a hundred years ago. In today's theatre, especially on Broadway, the design and execution of scenery to enhance a production in various ways is very important. Unless, of course, the director is determined to get down to basics and work only with a bare stage and black drapes. Appropriately conceived settings can suggest a sense of time, place, mood, and style. They can stress realism or open up a world of fantasy—or nightmare. Costumes are quite as important, although audiences are often not as conscious of the contribution they make to the total visual effect. Usually, the designers of sets and costumes are most successful when the spectators are not aware—after the first pleasure of seeing an impressive set—of their work. As designer Peter Harvey says, "No matter how remarkable the scenery may be, after fifteen minutes of looking at it, the audience loses interest and wants to see a play."

Some designers coordinate the style, the colors, the textures of sets and costumes by the simple solution of designing them both. Some even develop the lighting design as well, to make sure colored gelatines don't wash out the subtle colors of the sets and the gowns. More often, however, different designers will be responsible for sets, for costumes, for lights, and, now, even for sound—which includes musical backgrounds and sound effects. In some productions, such as a Western staging of a Kabuki drama, there may even be a makeup designer, with the responsibility of creating authentic traditional Kabuki makeup for actors not skilled enough to do it for themselves. A director might prefer to call this person a makeup coordinator. Whatever the title, when a show requires a number of unusual facial treatments in a consistent style, this cannot be left to individual performers to work out on their own.

Designers don't actually have to build what they design, although some will take up a brush or a needle when union rules don't forbid it. Their job, however, is largely—after consultation with the director to be sure that they understand his visualization of the play—to provide him with sketches and plans of the sets and costume plates indicating colors, fabrics, and accessories. Lighting and sound designers draw up plots for their instruments.

A lot of talent and skill are needed if you are to be successful as a theatre designer. You will have to work hard to get designing jobs. When you get them, there is even more hard work ahead. You may have to make some changes—even extensive ones—to please the director. When sets or costumes are being constructed, you will want to oversee the work, even though the actual building may be supervised by someone else. At rehearsals, you will want to make sure that everything looks right and works right. If it doesn't, you will find yourself involved in last-minute revisions or substitutions.

Although you may be able to do some designing in nonunion theatres, you will have to pass difficult examinations to be admitted to the United Scenic Artists. Present members are not eager to have more competition in a market without much work. There is also a $1,000 initiation fee. Getting design jobs isn't easy either. That's why some talented set and costume designers are willing to work for little or nothing on showcase productions. Their work will be seen, and the show might transfer to the commercial theatre, in which case they would receive the requisite union fee for their designs.

There are also fashions in designers. Some well-known artists may have several Broadway shows one season, but in the next couple of seasons no one may ask them to design a show. Of course, there is always the possibility of designing for the regional theatre, or even being invited to teach and design for a college drama department. A number of designers do other kinds of design work: interior design, product design. Some, if they have the right union card, even paint sets designed by other artists when they have no other work. Designing a major film may be more financially rewarding than a major play.

If you have original ideas about recreating fantasy or reality on stage, if you have a good sense of how to use elements of design, and if you love working in the theatre in some capacity, set and/or costume design may be the right answer for you. Classes in sketching, watercolors, and sculpting should be useful. Drafting is important if you are to draw gound plans and elevations. You might want to learn to build set models, although they are not always required by a director or producer. It could also be useful to get practical experience in building, painting, and lighting sets.

This you can do in school or community theatres.

Potential costume designers have to learn about the human body, how it is put together, how it moves. They must learn about fabrics:

textures, weaves, dyes, durability, ease of cleaning, how the cloth will drape or move on an actor. They need to learn how to draft patterns for costumes. Because a number of dramatic classics require costumes from other periods, a costume designer also needs to know the history of costume and how it relates to other aspects of life in a given period. In high school, home economics classes deal with some of this. At the college level, many schools with drama majors have both undergraduate and graduate courses devoted to important aspects of this training.

At the college level, the same is true of lighting, which sometimes has sound design and engineering problems thrown in. In high school, shop courses and physics classes can provide some useful basic information. But if you want to work as a designer, you need to get practical training by working on shows wherever and whenever you can. It's also helpful to get catalogues from major suppliers of lighting and sound equipment in order to become familiar with what is available to you to create special effects with light and sound.

Working professionally in any of the theatre arts or crafts requires union membership, but there are plenty of opportunities in nonunion situations. Theatre people always need well-trained technical talents. Whether they can pay a living wage is something else.

CHAPTER III

Your Career in Music Theatre, Dance, and Concerts

Who knows how many important careers in music and dance have been nipped in the bud by parents or teachers? "But why?" you may ask. "Don't our parents and our teachers want the best for us? Don't they want us to do well in the careers we choose?"

Of course they do! But sometimes children who really enjoy singing and dancing—if only to amuse themselves—are actively discouraged: "Would you *please* stop making that awful noise! I can't stand it any longer. You can't carry a tune." Or: "Just stop all that prancing around right this minute! What do you think you're doing? Your father would kill you if he saw you doing all that airy-fairy dancing!"

Often without thinking, parents manage to convince their children that they have no talent for musical performance. Sometimes a child is deeply hurt when an impatient or teasing parent tells him or her that singing is an impossibility. Some parents discourage their children on purpose. For some men, dancing is not a "manly" enough career for their sons to follow. Sometimes both parents may try to forestall a budding artist in the family out of real concern for his or her economic security: "You want to be an *opera* star? Well, that's very nice. But what will you do for a *living?*"

In fact, that's just what the parents of several important American opera stars said to them when they first thought of singing as a career. They said such things not because they didn't like music, but because they did not believe it would be possible for their children to make a living as singers. Fortunately, they were wrong, as the children have successfully proved.

But most discouragements are not intentional. A mother is impatient, a teacher is overworked, and out slips a remark that a student accepts as a final judgment: "You don't have to be in the chorus. You're such a montone that you'll throw everyone else off key."

If this has happened to you, don't think it means that a musical career is absolutely closed to you. It can do a lot to make you think you have no aptitude for music, but most people have more talent for music than is generally suspected. So if you feel strongly attracted to the world of music, you must try to overcome the prejudices others may have about your hopes. If you were discouraged as a child, you may already have lost valuable time in which you could have been preparing to work as a singer, an instrumentalist, or a dancer. Of course, it's not easy, if you are only five or six, to insist on having dance lessons, especially if your parents don't think they can afford them.

That is why many young people in their early teens can profit from more freedom of choice in junior high and high school courses. They can choose music and dance study, depending on how much is offered at their schools. If they have after-school jobs they can pay for their own music or dance lessons with a private teacher.

There are, it is true, several systems designed to teach young children musical skills. In Japan, amazing results have been achieved in getting groups of small children to play the piano and the violin with some ability. In Hungary, the composer Zoltán Kodály developed a system of teaching—not so force-fed as the Japanese—that makes the mysteries of the elements of music fairly easy to understand. Kodály's ideas are now being used in many countries, as is the system devised by the Bavarian composer Carl Orff.

To Carl Orff, creator of the dynamic music for the medieval song cycle *Carmina Burana,* we are all musical. Some more so than others, possibly, but we all have a sense of rhythm, an instinctive response to music and dancing. Orff has studied music from all over the world and collected instruments from many lands—instruments that he sometimes uses in composing and playing his own music. What has impressed him is some basic similarities in music and the way in which people respond to it no matter where they live.

The worst thing a teacher can do, he believes, is to tell a student that he or she has no musical talent. Perhaps, unlike Mozart, who was composing symphonies at five, the student hasn't yet composed an opera. But that doesn't mean the student doesn't have some potential to make—and to enjoy—music. So Orff likes to have children begin learning about music in a very easy, enjoyable way. Instead of a music lesson, it's more like recess time, because the Orff *Schul-Werk* or schoolwork often begins with some popular children's games. These games, of which there are variations in many lands, usually involve some kind of chanting or repetition of verses or choruses, as well as rhythmic movement. In fact, Orff and those who teach like him want to develop the whole person. Music isn't only an end in itself. Nor is movement, but a musician whose body does not respond at all to the beat and the pitch variations of the music he plays may turn out to be a really boring player. That's even more true of a singer.

In the Orff system, working in friendly groups, there is no stage fright, no harsh judgment about anyone's abilities, no pressure to do something remarkable right away. As work on games and songs continues, simple rhythm and percussion instruments are introduced, but no one is forced to play anything more than a pair of wood blocks until he is ready. If a student is dying to try the xylophone, of course he can do so. If he thinks he wants to go on to the piano, fine! But no one pushes him, and no one says he will be a failure before he tries.

Such teaching methods, though they are becoming increasingly popular, either under the Orff name or some other, are not yet universal. There are still teachers who won't have time for you unless you already show signs of great promise. But if you believe in yourself, you should be able to find a way. Granted, it's much easier in a big city than it is in a small town, for there are a lot more music teachers, choruses, bands, and other groups in which you can learn something valuable about music and dance.

In any case, it's useful to develop your musical skills, even if you do not pursue an active career, because there is so much pleasure to be gained from making your own music or playing it with friends. And, if there aren't thousands and thousands of Americans who love music, who understand it in some degree, then where will the audiences be for those who do go on to concert or opera or ballet careers?

Speaking of ballet careers, it is ironic that the decision to study ballet usually has to be made fairly young, sometimes before a child is really old enough to understand what is being proposed. So the decision is made by the parents for the child. The decision to study acting, on the other hand, can be made when a person is already mature. A number of acting teachers prefer to work with students who have "lived a little." It may even be a waste to spend too much time on acting technique when you are still in the middle teens. You could become too self-conscious, too affected.

Classical ballet, however, is different. The body has to be trained to respond in certain ways. The muscles, the bones, all the body's components, have to learn special movements and positions. These are not easy to master, but when they are mastered, you should be able to do them with the appearance of ease and grace. What you do as a dancer may be very difficult, but you mustn't let it look difficult.

Aside from social dancing and folk dance, many schools do not spend much time on discovering and developing the dance talents of their students. Dancing may be used as an aspect of physical education. It may even be related to some gymnastics exercises. That means that at the elementary school level, parents, not teachers, are usually the ones who decide that ballet lessons are important. At the high school level, the student may make the decision for himself or herself. Although some little ballet "rats" have begun at six years of age, a teen-age student willing to work hard can still develop into an impressive dancer.

For those who are more interested in working as dancers in musicals or in modern dance ensembles—not to mention doing dance routines in clubs and cabarets—college may not be too late to begin study. But the general rule is: the earlier you begin, the better. When your body and muscles are once used to moving in certain set ways, it's very hard to retrain them. It's not just force of habit that you move the way you do; trying suddenly to alter your movement patterns can be very painful.

So the dancer's study usually begins early in life; more so for classical ballet, however, than for other kinds of dance. The training is also very demanding. You really need to practice every day, to keep limber, to master the techniques, to improve your style. Such discipline is not for every child. Forced against your will, you are apt to rebel, and all the time and money will be wasted. Few teachers will bother long with a student who has been sent against his will. But if they see real talent, they may begin to encourage it and help change the student's attitude about dance study.

If you live in a town where the only dance instruction is given once in a while in gym class—usually new popular dances or some exotic folk dances from the Ukraine or Uganda—you probably won't go far in dance. But most towns today have at least one private teacher of dance, and some localities have a number of professional schools. If the sign on the school in your town says: "Miss Twinkletoes' Academy of the Ballet," you may have a problem. If all the classes seem to be filled with tiny girls in pink tutus, the school may simply be not geared to working with older students. Your best bet in finding a good dance teacher or a school in your community or near it would be to have your librarian get a copy of the *Dance Annual,* a yearly publication of *Dance* magazine, which lists teachers and schools all over the United States. If you want to learn more about various schools, teachers, choreographers, and dance ensembles, you should read issues of *Dance, Dance-Scope, Dance News,* and *Ballet News,* all of them devoted to the art of dance and the people who keep it alive and well.

We are talking about beginnings of study now, not advanced work.

And when you are thinking about beginnings, you need to think also about endings. It is sad but true that dancers, as a rule, do not have long careers. There comes a time in middle life, especially for dancers of classical ballet, when the body simply will no longer do the wonderful things it once did. That doesn't happen to every dancer, however. Some, through remarkable discipline, bodily strength, rigorous daily training, and indomitable will, continue to work. Alicia Alonso, of the Cuban National Ballet, was still dancing at sixty. Some change to less rigorous dance forms. Some, like the redoubtable Martha Graham, continue performing at some level of artistic movement into their seventies and eighties.

Fortunate is the dancer who has the patience and the love to become a good teacher. But not all good dancers are good teachers, although it's easier to teach dance movement than voice control. Some dancers become choreographers, creating ballets, modern dances, musical comedy numbers, or cabaret and television routines. Some take even more responsibility and not only choreograph but also organize and operate their own dance ensembles. When this occurs, they are often able to make an even greater contribution to dance life and culture than they did when they only danced. Still, the young would-be dancer has to face the fact that he may need a new career, possibly outside the dance world, sometime in his middle years.

Among music performers, the same thing is true only of singers. The great pianist Arthur Rubinstein began as a youthful prodigy and was still playing the piano with tremendous energy into his nineties. Instrumentalists can usually expect long performance careers, as long as they can find audiences to listen to them. But with singers, especially in demanding forms such as opera, a full, strong voice often begins to show signs of wear in middle age. Perhaps it's the singer's upper register that goes first; high notes become terribly shrill, off key, impossible. It may be that the lower notes become harder and harder to project. Only in the middle range is the singer still secure.

Operatic arias are often composed to show off the brilliance of a voice and the marvels of a singer's technique in using it. When hearing an aria becomes a torture rather than a pleasure, audiences and critics will say it's time for the singer to retire. Fortunately, popular music is much less demanding on the voice—and the intelligence, in some cases. Some beloved singers have created new careers singing less taxing songs, light classics and popular songs. Or, like talented dancers, they may become teachers. Curiously, a number of remarkable singers do not understand technically how they are able to sing so well, and they do *not* make good teachers. If you teach voice, you must be able to explain it. But if former singers cannot teach vocal control, production, resonance, and similar elements of voice training, they may still be able to coach young singers to interpret—phrasings, intonations, feelings, actions—the roles they have sung so well during their brilliant careers.

As with would-be actors, hopeful singers can begin their voice training rather later than dancers should. The voice needs to mature; in the early teens it is still developing and changing. That doesn't mean that participation in choruses or even singing solos will damage the voice. That kind of musical preparation and preliminary experience can be very helpful, not least in learning to read music and to perform in concert with others. Most musicians do not perform solo, so it's good to get used to the ways in which groups make music together.

As already noted, in Japan children are taught to play instruments such as the piano and violin when they are quite young. That is not in itself remarkable, because in America for many years families that could afford the lessons often forced at least one of the children—sometimes all of them—to study piano or violin. The problem for the young American piano student frequently was that he or she simply did not want to learn to play. Daily practice was boring—time taken away from real play. In many cases, children forced to study piano or violin gave up the instrument as soon as their parents stopped paying for lessons or making them practice. Sometimes the rest of the family was grateful the lessons had come to an end, since the noise of daily scales and badly played exercise pieces also was over. Some unwilling students did learn their lessons well, however, and today are glad that they can play an instrument. Some of them gradually came to love both music and the instrument and went on to be professional musicians. Others are satisfied with being able to play the piano at home for their own enjoyment or for friends. Or to be able to play with neighbors in an amateur string quartet, or even in a community band or orchestra.

If you were forced to study an instrument and made such a fuss about it that your parents or your teachers gave up, you may already realize that you made a mistake. But you can repair the damage by resuming study. Even adults who have never played an instrument can learn to do so. It is easier, however, if you begin younger, while the bones and muscles are developing. Obviously, when you are a child your fingers can't stretch an entire octave on the piano. You may find it difficult to finger the strings on a violin. But, making a start, you grow into mastery of the instrument and the techniques that make it come alive.

Music teachers often suggest the piano as the best instrument for a beginner and say that you can't start too young. But you shouldn't be forced to study; you should want to do it. That means that parents, friends, and teachers need to encourage you, to help you understand what a gift it is to be able to make music.

There are several advantages to learning to play the piano, regardless of what kind of musical career you later pursue. One is that it is a very versatile instrument, used in many ways. If you become a singer, you can use it to work out a new song or aria. You might accompany a ballet rehearsal, or even early stages of an opera rehearsal where the piano always takes the place of the large, expensive orchestra. You may become a singer's accompanist. You might use the piano in teaching voice privately or training a chorus in a high school. Learning to play the piano is an excellent drill in learning to read music. You have to read more than one line of music at a time: you read and play the left and the right hands' music simultaneously. Or you should, if you are doing it right. That's good preparation for being a conductor—some famous conductors are, in fact, excellent concert pianists—since a conductor may work from a musical score with as many as eighty lines in it, representing what each group of orchestral instruments is supposed to be playing.

Pianos are expensive, and not every family can afford to own one. So guitars are becoming popular beginning instruments with many teenagers. A guitar is inexpensive and easily portable. It is also the instrument of choice for many rock and pop stars. Elton John is one of the few who are pianists. For many who learn to play the guitar, the goal is purely pleasure, but for some the aim is success in popular music performance, either as part of a combo or as a soloist. Many attempt this; few succeed, and the price they have to pay in personal terms is sometimes much too high for the money they may make. Fame as a pop star can evaporate overnight. Fans grow older; tastes change rapidly.

The potential problem with the guitar is that many learn to play it only by ear. They can't actually read music for the guitar. And guitar music, since it has to be recorded in a series of chord diagrams, is different from piano music and sometimes harder to read. It's easier for a pianist to master the guitar than the other way around. That is not to say that the guitar is only an instrument for popular music. Andres Segovia and John Williams have brilliantly demonstrated how challenging the classical guitar can be.

There are no hard and fast rules about how you can become a musician. Prodigies usually need little or no training. Some dedicated people could study for years and never reach the level of Mozart at eight.

Even untrained genius finds a way of breaking through. It seems astounding, but the beloved American composer Irving Berlin, it's said, never learned to read music. He had a piano specially built so that he could work out tunes in one key and the piano could transpose them into other keys. Once a melody was set, Berlin could have someone else set it down in musical notation.

Musicians often advise young people to get involved in high school band and chorus, as well as community groups. Not only is there usually some formal class instruction connected with school music groups, but there is also the added challenge of learning to cooperate with others. Music is almost always a group effort.

Foreign languages can also be helpful, and not just for singers who hope to work on the opera stage or to give concerts of German *Lieder*, French art songs, and Spanish popular airs. Much of the concert and opera repertoire comes from Europe, especially Western Europe. Not only are the words often sung in the original language, instead of English, but the musical markings are frequently also in that language; it helps if the musician is able to understand them.

Singers with major careers fly all over the world to fulfill solo, orchestral, and opera engagements. Major symphony orchestras and special small ensembles such as baroque and chamber groups often tour in foreign lands. Many governments prefer to send a symphony abroad on a goodwill tour rather than a drama troupe, because music is said to speak an international language that doesn't need to be translated. It also isn't easy to take political offense from music, whereas a play can cause trouble. Foreign language study can also be valuable to those who work in popular music. Pop groups and soloists also tour widely, thanks to the instant worldwide reputations records and cassette tapes have given them. Elton John even went to play in Russia, which has long condemned the pop music of the West.

What applies to musicians and singers also applies to dancers. When an American ensemble such as Alwin Nikolais's troupe or Alvin Ailey's is performing in Germany, it's a big help if the dancers and technicians know some German, especially music, dance, and theatre technology terms. As an American artist abroad, you cannot expect everyone to speak English to you; not in their own lands. If you are so lucky as to be given a contract to join the ensemble of the Bavarian State Opera in Munich, for example, you'd better be able to speak German off the stage as well as sing it on stage. One reason so many Americans have begun their opera careers in Germany—aside from the important fact that World War II had devastated German ensembles—was that the Americans were eager to learn German and indeed learn anything they were asked to. This eagerness and flexibility, not often seen in the European artists at that time, was much admired and valued by European conductors and directors. It still is.

Music, as notated and as played, involves a kind of mathematics. Studying trigonometry won't be much help, but simple mathematics certainly will help in understanding some of music's measurements and relationships. In addition to basic music courses, a grounding in the humanities is of value. Music teachers and musicians may disagree about the value of a college degree, but most do insist that some acquaintance with the cultures and histories from which has come much of our serious and ethnic folk music can only help in learning to interpret it effectively. Even special music schools such as the famed Juilliard in New York have humanities studies in their curricula.

If you are interested in a classical music career, as a singer or an instrumentalist, you will need daily practice for some years before you are ready for professional work. You might as well be doing this practice in the framework of a college education, if your college has a good music faculty. You don't necessarily have to get a degree, but the guidance of good teachers in an atmosphere dedicated to study will be good for you. Fortunately, many colleges have excellent music staffs, because teaching is one important way a good musican can make a living. Learning to play an instrument, of course, is much more than just getting the notes right. That's fairly simple. What needs your mastery is interpretation: Should this passage be played faster, slower? Louder? Softer? With a light or a heavy attack? With love or with ferocity?

Do not imagine, however, that you will get into any college music department just by announcing that that is your intention or your right. Most require an audition first. Most expect you to be fairly proficient on at least one instrument. You must of course be able to read music, although some schools do offer remedial work in that.

Some very gifted young musicians go from high school to leading music schools like Juilliard, Curtis, or Peabody. Others may have some college training first. Juilliard is regarded by many as the best music school in America at present. It is very expensive, because leading teachers and teacher/performers give individual instruction in voice and on instruments. Fortunately, at Juilliard and other major schools, a number of scholarships are usually available for talented students who otherwise couldn't afford such studies.

Juilliard is not for everyone with talent. The competition is very stiff. For some students, the shock of moving from a Midwestern town of 5,000 to New York City with its millions is unsettling enough without having to face fierce competition from fellow students. For some who feel they must ultimately come to New York to polish their training, it may be better to come "by degrees," moving from a small-town teacher and high school band to a larger college music department and then to a school in a moderate-sized city in the heartland. Music educators emphasize that many fine, experienced musicians do not care to live in New York, even though it is the acknowledged center of America's musical life. They prefer to teach and perform in smaller cities or communities, and this is why so many colleges now have outstanding music faculties. Often, there is just not enough professional performance work in such locales, and teaching rounds out the musician's income.

Training, whether for instrumentalists, dancers, or singers, is always a question involving some relativity. Some teachers are better than others. Some are very good with some students and disastrous with other students. Some teachers are downright charlatans. But how is the beginning student to know which is which? Colleges and schools have accreditation processes that should guarantee the excellence of their faculties. But with private teachers, it's a different matter. Few teachers want to be put in the position of condemning fellow teachers. That is a knife that can easily cut both ways.

Both musicians and music educators are apt to tell you that you have finally to judge for yourself whether your chosen teacher is really helping you. If you find you are not getting along at any level of work and communication, clearly you should find a different teacher. Sometimes the pupil-teacher chemistry just doesn't work, though the student has talent and the teacher is a master. But just because the teacher is tough on you, don't think he's not good. He is probably trying to teach you discipline, good work habits. A teacher who says you are a wonderful musician when you know your playing or vocalizing is not very good is probably not going to help you much. Also, teachers can be wrong. Some musicians have made careers for themselves even though teachers despaired of them, dismissed them. If you are determined, you may become a self-made artist. After all, there is no prescribed age at which a piano student has to make a debut. It could be at six, at sixteen, or even at thirty-six—though that's putting things off a bit.

Just as dancers need to find a teacher who can give them what they need, so, too, do singers need to find the right teacher. Some established singers also make a distinction between their *teacher* and their *coach.* It may seem odd—not only that a singer feels the need of two experts to help, but that, already launched in a professional career, the singer still takes lessons. Not at all. Dedicated musicians need to practice every day just to keep the skills they have. And they need to master music they have not played or sung before. A singer is always working on the voice. New operatic roles offer new challenges. A new concert program also requires a lot of preparation. In music and dance, unlike many areas of college study, you must not stop studying just because you have finished the course-work and earned a degree. (Surveys show that some students of English or history seldom read a serious book, especially in those fields, after college.)

Voice teachers are primarily concerned with helping students develop their vocal mechanisms, mastering technical production of sound. They are interested in such elements as pitch, purity of tone, volume, resonance and timbre, projection, tempo, modulation. Of course, some teachers are also coaches, but a coach specializes in interpretation of vocal music, whether it be operatic roles, oratorios, or song cycles. Such matters as pronunciation, phrasing, intonation, and emotion are important to the coach.

Today, we know a lot about the physics of sound, about the mechanism of the human voice. So if a teacher starts talking about the "mystical properties" of the voice, you'd better find another teacher. Voice teachers aren't licensed; they don't have to pass a state examination. In some cases, they don't even have to get results. If you don't progress, they may tell you it's your fault, not theirs. That may not be true.

With the inexpensive recording devices now available, there's little excuse for you to be deaf to your own vocal improvement or lack of it. But you shouldn't work with a cassette-recorder all the time; it's not full-fidelity; you don't sound exactly like that to others. You can be a better judge of what you play on the piano or violin than you can of your voice. We don't hear ourselves the way others do, so a tape now and then can be a good way to check. It can also be an interesting aid for an instrumentalist who records a study piece today and then again six months later to see what changes, what improvements have been made. (Dancers can profit from watching their work on videotape.)

A lot of young people who are interested in music careers begin by hoping to emulate the solo success of some idol, either in the field of serious music or popular. The truth is that there is very little room at the top. But there is always room for the very gifted, the very well trained, the very aggressive and ambitious. An important career in serious music, which includes the classical and the avant-garde, can be longer-lasting and its fame more enduring than pop stardom. The financial rewards of the instant will probably be nowhere as great in serious music, but over the years a major instrumental soloist or a singer can become quite prosperous. In popular music, reputations are often achieved through publicity and promotion, aided by fads and fashions that have little to do with solid talent or hard-earned technique. That's why some pop stars have burned out so abruptly, never to be heard of again. It isn't easy to keep the fickle public's affection over the years, even if you are a good musician, so anyone who wants a career in the more commercial aspects of music should know what the risks are.

Some lovers of equality hate such terms as "serious" or "classical" music. They usually hate that kind of music as well, but their objections are often based on the idea that all music is equally good. Therefore, we should give Bob Dylan's music as much serious respect as we do Beethoven's. You can get into a lot of unprofitable arguments about definitions and classifications in the world of music. Obviously, some rock lyrics are so mindless that no one could seriously call them serious. On the other hand, many of Dylan's or Joan Baez's fans would be understandably angry if you said they weren't serious about their music. Perhaps it's easier to think of such clearly popular, commercially successful compositions as music that appeals to the many, creations that often in both lyrics and music are not as complex, as challenging as most serious music.

It might be considered patronizing to refer to serious music as that which does not make money or appeal to a mass audience. This may make it sound "elitist," but the truth is that performing the classics and avant-garde works often costs more than can be earned by ticket sales. Concerts by famous soloists are a notable exception. Opera production requires tremendous subsidies before a season can even be planned or tickets printed. Symphony orchestras customarily also need subsidy, and rising wages for musicians and increasing touring costs indicate that even more donations will be needed. It is true that some ensembles, through very careful budgeting and lucrative contracts for tapes and records, can manage to break even, but even these usually also have generous patrons.

Rising costs are hurting some established musical groups now. Seasons, tours, personnel have been cut back. Some ensembles have merged with nearby groups. Some have disbanded. At the same time, however, in many cities and towns new groups are forming. Opera workshops are springing up everywhere, and dance ensembles are numerous, almost too numerous for the available dance public. Even in the performing arts, the law of supply and demand may be seen to operate. There certainly are jobs, but the market fluctuates. Those eager music students who once hoped for stardom may have to settle for a chair as second violinist or a place in the opera chorus. And they may be lucky to land those jobs.

Bill Boswell, a young pianist-conductor-composer who also teaches music at Brooklyn College, points out that a good violinist in a symphony orchestra can make better money than many car salesmen. Such a job can be a secure living, musical, fulfilling, creative, he says. "We don't all have to be Steve Sondheim or Leonard Bernstein," he stresses. "The Cliburns and the Menuhins get all the attention, but they represent a very small percentage of all those who work in music."

WORKING IN MUSIC AND DANCE

To give you an idea of the scope of some major music and dance organizations—similar to ones in which you might find a position if you do not pursue a career as a solo instrumentalist—here are some lists of positions. The first one is for the New York City Opera, just across Lincoln Center Plaza from the Metropolitan Opera. It doesn't have the budget or the season that the Met has, but its achievements in opera production have been admired internationally. It has been a nurturing place for young American talent. An unknown soprano in its ranks rose to become one of its stars, after which she was invited to make her debut at the Met. When she retired from singing, she became the City Opera's first woman director. She is, of course, Beverly Sills.

This list of City Opera positions is limited to those for which musical training is mandatory or desirable. There are a number of jobs, artistic, administrative, and technical, for which you would not have to have a music background, though it could be helpful.

New York City Opera: Director, Managing Director, Associate Managing Director, Director of Operations, Production Coordinator, Company Manager, Tour Coordinator, Assistants, Music Administrator, Director of Musical Studies and Educational Programs, Associate Music Administrator, Assistant Music Administrator, Rehearsal Assistant, Chorus Master, Assistant, Director of Children's Chorus, Orchestra Personnel Manager, Assistant, Librarian, Director of Ballet, Assistant, Staging Staff Administrator, Director of Supers, Assistant, Assistant for Chorus Staging, Language Coach, Producer, Radio-TV Broadcasts.

Then there are the Music Staff (13 members), the Director/Staging Staff (16 members, not full-time), the Choreographers (4, only 1 full-time), followed by the actual artists: Sopranos (29 singers), Mezzos (14 singers), Tenors (22 singers), Baritones/Basses (31 singers), Child

Sopranos and Trebles (4 singers), Solo Dancers (4 dancers), Actor (1, in a speaking role), Conductors (9 conductors), Concert Master (only 1 in each orchestra), First Violins (12), Second Violins (11), Violas (7), Cellos (6), Basses (5), Flutes (3), Piccolo (1), Oboes (3), English Horn (1), Clarinets (3), Bass Clarinet (1), Bassoons (3), Contra Bassoon (1), Horns (5), Trumpets (3), Tuba (1), Harp (1), Tympani (1), and Percussion (2). Not enumerated here are the chorus and the corps de ballet.

That may look like an impressive roster of musical or music-oriented jobs—and it doesn't include all the performing arts jobs at the City Opera. But the roster of artists at the Met is even larger. The New York Philharmonic Orchestra, since it doesn't have to do its work cramped into a small orchestra pit beneath the apron of a stage, has a larger complement of musicians.

One of the most successful films made about ballet was *Turning Point,* which deals with the difficult decisions dancers have to make about careers versus personal lives. It was made with the assistance of American Ballet Theatre, which was long headed by two Directors, Lucia Chase and Oliver Smith, assisted by two Associate Directors, Antony Tudor and Nora Kaye. In its 1979 season it starred twenty leading dancers, including Fernando Bujones, Cynthia Gregory, Anthony Dowell, Natalia Makarova, Gelsey Kirkland, Rudolf Nureyev, and Martine van Hamel. Some eighteen talented dancers were featured, and the corps de ballet numbered forty-nine enthusiastic young ballet dancers. One of the corps, Lise Houlton, when she was on her home ground in Minneapolis with the Minnesota Dance Theatre, performed as a leading dancer.

Other positions in ABT which require either dance or musical training or both are: Assistant Director, Regisseur, Ballet Master (3 masters), Music Director, Associate Conductor, Ballet Mistress, and, in the Rehearsal Department, Associate Ballet Master, Ballet Mistress, Assistant Ballet Mistress, Rehearsal Coordinator, and Choreologist—who notes down the choreography for new ballets in Benesh Notation. In the Music Department there are four company pianists. (There are, of course, capable administrative officers, a hard-working staff, a Financial Department, and a large, well-trained Production Department, responsible for preparing and presenting the ballets. The American Ballet Theatre also has a School. Including its director, it has a teaching staff of five, with one pianist. It also has a Ballet Repertory Company, with three administrators.

If the idea of being an opera star, a prima ballerina, or a solo flutist to rival Jean-Pierre Rampal is still your goal, instead of working in the ranks, with the musical or dance "committee," well and good. But don't forget how few openings there are in opera production. Today, the European opera theatres that once clamored for young American talent have plenty of young professionals of their own. Also, it's no longer enough to be able to sing well. Modern opera performers are expected to be accomplished actors and dancers as well. If there is a court ball, they should be able to take a role in it and not look like wallpaper while the opera ballet does a three-minute sequence. One good thing about opera and dance for those who believe women haven't had equal opportunity in many areas of art and work is that women feature prominently in major and minor roles. Only now are more jobs opening up for women in orchestras and smaller ensembles.

Even if you are a fine pianist or singer, there is no law requiring Columbia Artists Management to offer you a U.S. tour, or even a New York debut. Many would-be instrumental soloists and vocalists have to hire Town Hall, Alice Tully Hall, or Carnegie Recital Hall themselves if they are to have a New York debut. If you live in Cleveland, Indianapolis, or Provo, that may seem an unnecessary expense. Why bother about a New York debut? Who cares in Ohio, Indiana, or Utah?

If that's your performance horizon, fine. But without a New York debut *and* favorable reviews, national tours and bookings around the U.S. are problematic. Much of the booking is done out of New York, though now there are more regional touring managements. Even having a New York debut doesn't guarantee that any music critics will come or that they will like your performance.

In New York City, there are some 25,000 members of the American Federation of Musicians, so there is no shortage of brilliant instrumentalists. In fact, some experts think there are entirely too many talented young pianists for the available jobs as orchestra soloists and for the potential audience for solo concerts. Arthur Rubinstein has told the story of one of his students who proudly came to tell him that he had just won the Queen Elizabeth of Belgium competition. "Oh?" said Rubinstein to his student. "Were the others so bad?" Rubinstein has said that in any period a country only needs six to ten excellent pianists or violinists. The recording industry certainly helps focus public attention on the performances of a limited group of noted artists. The problem for a young soloist, then, is to manage to have the important debuts, the good reviews, the concert bookings, the orchestral invitations, and the recording contracts. That is why personal publicity and management have become so important to young artists as well as to those who are well established.

A century ago a musician who could play the fantastically difficult compositions of Franz Liszt was sometimes said to have a gift from the Devil. Today any instrumentalist should be able to do that. If he cannot, he is inadequate and shouldn't expect to have a career even in an orchestra. Such jobs are won by audition—obviously the conductor has to hear you play—but résumés and past experience are also indicative of who you are and what you've accomplished so far.

A different psychology is involved in being an orchestra member, as opposed to being a soloist. You are a member of the group and need to work well with them. Pay is generally good, and you are less exposed as an artist. But unless you are with one of the major American symphony orchestras, you had better be prepared to travel a lot. Small ensembles spend most of their time on the road. That kind of music-making may mean wearing "tails" six times a week, living out of a suitcase, traveling long hours in buses, and spending only one night in each town. If you have a family, you will often have to be absent from them.

Today most of the players in the New York Philharmonic could have been outstanding soloists. Musicians are getting better and better. They can read more difficult music, respond to more unusual musical challenges, and generally show a more versatile technical mastery of their instrument. That means that competition for a vacant chair in that orchestra is very stiff indeed. If you want to join the Philharmonic or some other American symphony, you can find out when a chair becomes vacant by reading the *International Musician,* the official publication of the American Federation of Musicians (AFM). This is an important source of job information. Playing in the Philharmonic is a full-time job and very well paid, thanks to aggressive representation by the AFM at contract time. But that doesn't mean that a dedicated clarinetist might not fill in at a Bar Mitzvah or a birthday party if the hours and the pay were satisfactory. Capable musicians are able to perform more than one kind of music. Some play the classics for a living and jazz to relax.

If you believe your voice is not going to permit you a concert or opera career, you may opt for an opera chorus, an oratorio chorus, or even a small vocal ensemble such as the Gregg Smith Singers, Western Wind, or the Sine Nomine Singers. Some churches pay soloists quite well, as they do their organists. There is work in popular music in groups on TV shows. Performing as back-up singers for radio or TV commercials pays quite well. But very few singers aspire to be in a chorus.

A dancer's career usually begins in the corps—like a chorus—of the ballet unless he works with a very small ensemble and is featured quite early. Few singers ever step out of the opera chorus, however, to become stars of the Met. A musician has jokingly said that second violinists are happier playing second fiddle than choristers are backing up opera stars. But there is some truth in it. Actually, in America, there is very little full-time work for choristers. Most of it is part-time; a lot of it is really semiprofessional, unpaid, volunteer artistry. If you plan to practice your musical talents only as an avocation, making your money in another kind of profession, singing in a chorus can be very satisfying.

Some musicians, recognizing the importance of the recording industry to all kinds of music and audiences, have made careers in recording not as artists, but as technicians, directors, and managers. The alert, inventive artist can always find new ways to use his talents.

This covers the generalities, though not in the detail you will find in books devoted to specific aspects of opera, dance, and music. There are, however, some specific posts or roles in the worlds of these arts that deserve to be given brief special mention. Among them are the positions of the men who run opera and dance ensembles and orchestras. In the opera house, the chief may be called the Intendant (in Europe), the Artistic Director, or even the General Manager. The man in charge of the musical aspects of opera production is often called the General Music Director. With a symphony, he may be called the Music Director and Principal Conductor. Artistic Administrators audition, select, and help contract artists. Music Administrators or Music Secretaries oversee various aspects of programming and scheduling, both of rehearsals and performances, to make sure all runs smoothly.

Conductors and Assistant Conductors. Small music ensembles usually don't have conductors; one of the group gives the beat. Until the time of Haydn and Mozart, in fact, the harpsichordist conducted from the keyboard. Although some notable modern conductors such as Leonard Bernstein, Andre Previn, and Michael Tilson Thomas began as pianists, this doesn't mean that the harpsichordist turned into the conductor. Actually, the first violinist, who is today also the Concert Master, gradually took the tempo-setting function away from the keyboard musician, becoming the conductor. Now, however, the firmly established position of leadership as conductor can go to any instrumentalist who has the skill and stamina to coordinate all the elements of an orchestra. A really good conductor must understand the music, the instruments, the psychology of the players—and of the audience—and know how to blend all those into a moving performance. The ones who can do so lead America's major orchestras and those of Europe. Few began their musical careers determined to conduct. Most were first successful instrumentalists who gradually moved into conducting. It's true that some inadequate instrumentalists try to become conductors. Few college students who insist on studying conducting, rather than first mastering an instrument, are effective conductors.

Major conductors are very busy men, so Assistants are needed to rehearse the orchestras. Complicated works, including choruses, for instance, may have to be rehearsed in segments before they are all put together. If the Music Director is in charge of both the Boston and San Francisco Symphonies, as has happened, it is very important to have a good staff of assistants in both cities. Sometimes a distinguished guest conductor flies in only shortly before the concert. If new or difficult works are to be played, the orchestra must have rehearsed them well in advance.

Concert Master. He should be the best violinist in the entire orchestra, because he is responsible for the way the strings sound. He can also help the conductor set the interpretation of a work. In concert, though it may look as though he is giving the pitch to the rest of the players, this is actually done by an oboeist—since that sound is pure, with almost no overtones.

Music Librarian. His is not a full-time job unless the position is in a music archive or a university library. In a symphony orchestra, he may be one of the bassists or a second violinist. In an opera orchestra, he might be an assistant conductor or an accompanist. His job, for which he is paid extra, is to make sure that the parts for each piece to be played are placed on the stands of each player and, after performance, are collected and locked up. No orchestra will take the chance of letting players keep their own music. What if the tuba player loses his part on the way to the concert hall?

Language Coach. For this post, one should be at least a pianist, if not also a singer. In performance, it's not just a matter of singers pronouncing foreign words correctly. In fact, in singing them, the words are sometimes pronounced with some differences from speaking. In any case, singers do not sing individual words. Words have to be linked logically, emotionally, musically into understandable phrases that fit the musical setting. After all, they represent human emotion and thought being communicated. Coaches may have private studios for working with singers, or they may be engaged by opera companies. Good ones are always busy. Interestingly, some noted singers who are celebrated for certain roles in languages not their own may have learned the roles phonetically and actually not speak the languages well—or at all.

Choreographer. Someone must create the ballets and dances for dancers to perform; often the choreographer in ballet is a former dancer.

In modern dance, he or she may be the leading dancer or artistic director of the troupe. It isn't enough to piece together a series of steps, movements, and postures. A good choreographer must have the imagination to conceive a dance as a totality, visually striking, musically effective. Some traditional classical ballets have been passed on by ballet masters and leading dancers who have taught them to other dancers through rigorous rehearsals. But until the advent of inexpensive movie cameras and portable videotaping, a number of ballets and dances, once out of a company's repertoire, were forgotten. Or they could be revived only with difficulty, since even the original choreographer had forgotten exactly what happened in the ballet. There are dance notation systems such as Laban and Benesh notation, but trained experts are not plentiful or inexpensive.

Ballet Master/Mistress. Only the unremitting hard work and idealistic performance standards of these dedicated artist/teachers keep ballet companies at a high level of excellence. They are the unseen workers who, day after day, put the company through its paces, keep the bodies limber, shape and develop dancers, maintain the company repertoire, and help dancers master new choreography currently being set for them. The image in plays and films has been of a very stern, severe old dancer or former prima ballerina, remembering past glories and driving young dancers relentlessly on to be great stars. Certainly they want the best for their dancers, but they are often themselves in the prime of life. The ability to teach dance is what matters most, to be able to coordinate the rehearsal efforts of a large group.

Lyricist/Librettist. In the musical theatre, whether the form be opera, operetta, or musical comedy, the librettist is responsible for the "book" or text of the drama that is acted and sung. It's good if he is a musician or at least understands music, especially if he is also the lyricist, who must be a mixture of poet, playwright, and musician. The talents of a poet-playwright are more important in opera, where the text, both what may be spoken and what is sung, is often written in poetic form. In operetta or musicals, the spoken text is usually supposed to sound like natural speech. Few composers are like Richard Wagner, who created his own poetic texts for his opera scores. Or like Stephen Sondheim, who is a brilliant composer-lyricist. Both lyricists and librettists have to learn to think both musically and dramatically. Working in the musical theatre is the best place to learn to do that.

Composer. The range of possibilities for a composer is immense. He or she can compose for solo instrument, for solo instrument backed up by orchestra, for full symphony orchestra, for quartets, for chamber group, for chorus, for solo voice, and combinations of voice and orchestra and dancers, as in opera or musical comedy. There are many musical forms in which a composer can work. It is worth noting how many composers who have created primarily for instrumentalists have felt it necessary at least to try their skill at composing an opera. The music theatre certainly has its seductions for composers. Today, it is not regarded as a disgrace for a serious composer such as Leonard Bernstein to be eminently successful as a composer of hit Broadway shows such as *Candide* and *Wonderful Town.* Nor is it surprising any longer to find Broadway composers such as Richard Adler *(Damn Yankees)* or Charles Strouse *(Annie)* writing for symphony orchestras and the opera stage. One of the biggest critical quarrels about Stephen Sondheim's impressive work for the Broadway music theatre, *Sweeney Todd,* was whether it was just a musical or, in fact, an opera.

Orchestra/Arranger. Perhaps the composer is too busy to do more than work out the melodic line of a new composition? Then he needs an arranger to give it viable musical form and an orchestrator to decide how it can most effectively be played by the various instruments of an orchestra. Busy composers who know their craft very well often provide detailed musical sketches so that the orchestrator's work is comparatively simple. Some who are brilliant at conceiving new themes and melodies—especially for musical comedy—may not be so secure in their knowledge of what an orchestra can do; these composers need to lean heavily on good orchestrators. A few of them could do all the work available on Broadway in most seasons. The pay is good, but there are no royalties and not much acclaim. Television specials often need the services of good orchestrators who can work very fast. Two or three specials may be taped back-to-back, each with four or five new musical numbers, all of which must be orchestrated effectively.

And, of course, there always have to be those trained musicians who prompt the singers and copy music. Unsung heroes of music!

It is a wonderful satisfaction to be able to read music, to play an instrument, to sing well. For many who have studied music seriously but who work in other jobs and professions, this satisfaction is justification enough for their studies. But if you are determined to make a career in music, you should be prepared for much hard work and a certain amount of disappointment, depending on how good your talent and your training are. Many young musicians come to think that New York must be their eventual goal. That may be a real mistake, not only because there is professional work in Los Angeles as well, thanks to the film, television, and recording industries there, but because there is also professional work in many cities and towns in America. The challenge, the competition is frequently less, and that may be better for you. You have to make the decision. If you do go to New York and find that you cannot make a place for yourself in its rich music life, then have the courage to go home and make a good, solid career there—or in a less competitive city than New York.

The New York *Times* has reported that New York has at least 2,000 concerts a year, 25,000 members in the local of the American Federation of Musicians, not to mention visiting guest soloists, three major conservatories, and several college music programs. Its report was titled: *For New York's Musicians, Life May Often Play a Dirge* (March 30, 1979). What the *Times* discovered is that the very richness of the city's music life is what attracts so many musicians from elsewhere in America and from abroad. Only London's musical life can compare. That means that the opportunity to play with the best musicians, even if it isn't full-time, is worth it to many. So they find other jobs to support themselves, often completely outside the world of music. Some teach English; some drive taxis; some sell airline tickets; one clips news items for a newspaper morgue. All of these musicians would rather live and work that way than give up even the small degree of involvement they have in New York's world of music.

CHAPTER IV

Your Career in Technical Theatre

Stage fright is not just a problem for beginning actors. Many famed professionals admit to periodic attacks, especially on opening nights of new productions. If you have found this to be a problem, even with so light a challenge as having to give a five-minute speech in class, it need not mean that you should avoid a theatre career. You can still make an important contribution to the living theatre and never have to know a moment's terror of the audience or the blinding spotlights. If you are a technical worker, whether in the construction shops or backstage helping to run a production, you probably will never have to experience that awful moment in an actor's life when, with an audience of hundreds staring at him, he "dries up" and forgets what he must say next.

That doesn't mean that you can hide out backstage either. To make a living in the theatre, no matter how you do it, you usually have to work a little bit harder than your friends in other professons or occupations. There are a variety of material and psychic compensations for almost everyone who works in the performing arts to offset some of the very real disadvantages, but these compensations are not to be enjoyed by those who do not bring dedication, discipline, energy, and a sense of comradeship to their jobs.

In recent years, especially in Socialist or Communist countries, theatre, dance, and opera ensembles have often been treated—or even organized—as "collectives." The idea of a collective is that all the members who work in it, no matter what kind of jobs they have, should all have a say in what the group does and how it does it. In some circumstances, this has been carried to ridiculous extremes, with members insisting that all those involved must have an equal vote—which can mean that the ushers or the office receptionist have just as much right to choose the plays the company will produce as the theatre's artistic director.

In Sweden, where variations on this idea are popular, the result can be that a week of rehearsal time is wasted while the actors and even the designers argue with the director on how the play ought to be done. Making sure that everyone has been consulted can also use up a lot of valuable work time. Interestingly, in Communist countries, where the worker is supposed to be able to decide what his collective will do, the authority of the artistic director is still very clear. Of course, talented intendants, or theatre director/managers, make efforts to consult with colleagues to get their thinking on programs and productions. But men such as Joachim Herz in East Germany and Liviu Ciulei in Bucharest know that someone has to be in charge if a theatre is to operate successfully. As President Harry Truman used to say: "The buck stops here!" Someone has, finally, to make the major decisions for the ensemble and be willing to be responsible for the consequences.

That can give his colleagues a real feeling of security, so valuable to those involved in artistic enterprises. The performers, it's true, do not have total protection. If the audience doesn't like the intendant's final decisions on how the play should be acted, they may let the actors know it by booing or even throwing things. But if you are a worker in the technical side of theatre operation, you don't have to face that. Did you ever hear of a seamstress, back in the costume shop, being booed on opening night because a zipper failed? True, the next day the director might give her some notes she wouldn't soon forget, but that's not quite the same as having instant criticism on stage.

Thus, technical workers are in a much more protected position in serving the arts of music, dance, opera, and drama. But that doesn't mean they are totally free from pressure while on the job. The circumstances—occasionally chaotic—of much commercial and nonprofit theatre production are often such that a great deal of pressure is put on carpenters, painters, seamstresses, and other artisans. Sets and costumes frequently have to be constructed in record time, requiring long hours and uncertain schedules. And then, once they are seen on stage, a director or a designer may suddenly decide that drastic changes must be made immediately. It's not so unusual for a pre-Broadway show to drop $60,000 worth of scenery in Boston if the director thinks it's not effective.

Seasoned technical people are accustomed to such sudden changes and demands on their time and skills. When the production is commercial, union regulations guarantee that all will be fairly paid for the time and expertise they contribute. When the productions are amateur, however, technical workers must expect long hours, concentrated work sessions, great pressure, sometimes almost impossible demands on their ingenuity, and little or no financial reward for the time, energy, and imagination expended. Those who enjoy working in community or college theatre are used to this and find their reward in the satisfaction of a job well done and in the opportunity to work creatively with a group of fellow artists and artisans.

This sense of comradeship, of working together on something very special and wonderful, is not to be minimized. In many cases, it is the major compensation for working in the performing arts, rather than the monetary one. There are, it is true, theatre technicians who look on their work as virtually no different from a nine-to-five job on an assembly line. For such people, the variety and unpredictability of the theatre can be very annoying.

It's one thing to put your tools away at 5 P.M. and leave an assembly line, forgetting all about work until the next morning. It's quite a different matter to be getting ready to leave the theatre shop at 5 P.M. only to have someone rush in and tell you you've got to work overtime because some of the sets have just been destroyed in a traffic crash on their way from the shop to the theatre. (Very few professional, commercial theatres have shops in the same building as the actual theatre.) This may seem an extreme case, but crises are frequent in theatre production.

In recent years, producers, directors, and even performers have often criticized theatre craft unions for their fairly rigid rules about work hours, rates of pay, and jurisdiction. It is true that wage scales are often better for the crafts than for the performers, which is certainly discouraging to actors who may feel their work is more important than that of the man who merely raises the curtain. Still, those who are experts in their theatre crafts firmly believe that they should be paid what they think their skills are worth.

A source of some irritation to directors and actors have been union requirements regarding production work on stage. Sometimes an actor may find himself in a dispute with a stagehand if he has decided to speed things up—or be useful—and bring a chair onto the stage himself. The stagehand will probably insist that moving chairs is what he is paid to do, and the performer should let him do his job. He moves chairs and does not try to act to make himself "useful." On occasion, directors have been known to object to union insistence that electricians tend to their lighting and leave the chairs to the stagehands—and vice versa. But consider what a lot of trouble and expense could be caused if a director, without thinking, asked a stagehand—not trained as an electrician—to unplug a cord or move a lighting instrument. What if a short circuit occurred and a fire broke out? What if the man were seriously shocked, or even electrocuted?

That is why unions insist on rules and regulations. They have been evolved over the years for the protection of the workers: to protect them in regard to safety, possible overwork, and fair compensation. Anyone who has ever worked as a technician in amateur theatre has probably had experiences in which a demanding or unthinking director has asked him to do something that was unsafe or that he was not qualified to do. Not to mention asking him to work long hours for no pay.

What has annoyed producers and directors is a kind of featherbedding in which certain unions have determined just how many men should be employed in various job categories in specific commercial theatres for legitimate and musical productions. Sometimes, some of these jobs require little or no work, since a production that is renting a theatre may not need the services of some of the theatre's union-mandated technical staff; Broadway productions have their own tech staffs. Still, they are there to see that the interests of the theatre building are protected so that it will be ready to receive another production when the present one has closed or moved on.

In America, the sense of working in theatre as part of a collective, shared activity is often fragmented in the commercial sector, though much less so in amateur and professional regional theatres. In Europe, aside from London's West End commercial theatres or the boulevard theatres of Paris, most of the theatre activity is generated by state- or city-subsidized theatres. It is thoroughly professional, but it is not commercial in the sense of making profit. It is, in fact, expected to lose money; hence the subsidy. Such theatres, like the Residence Theatre in Munich, which is the Bavarian state theatre for drama, or Stockholm's Royal Opera, usually have all their technical shops in the theatre building complex itself or very close by. Thus, performers and technicians are working side by side in a real sense. At noontime in the theatre canteen, a music-loving scene painter may have a cup of coffee with a noted soprano and discuss her interpretation of some major opera roles. One very famous soprano is also famous for enjoying a spirited game of poker with members of the tech staff during breaks in rehearsal or performance.

There is less of that kind of comradeship in the Broadway theatre than in most other commercial, professional theatres in America. The simple reason for this is that almost all of the commercial theatres were built to get the maximum number of seats for the audience on prime midtown Manhattan real estate. The lobbies are usually ridiculously small, as are most of the lounges. Stages and wing space are equally cramped, not to mention the dressing-room space for the performers. Some star dressing rooms are scandalously small, with the lesser spaces even smaller.

That means that those who work on scenery and costume construction for many commercial theatre productions have little or no contact with the actual theatre in which the show will be performed, and thus also little contact with their performing colleagues. Construction shops have to be located in less expensive areas. Those technicians who must be present backstage or out in front to help run the show are more fortunate. They are a very visible part of the production team. Some enjoy that feeling of being part of a theatre production. To others it's just a job, though a bit different, perhaps, from building a house or installing a fuse box.

Even in some amateur and regional nonprofit theatres, some of the technical people who help prepare a show for production have little contact with the performers because shops are also located some distance from the theatre. Now, however, when a new theatre complex is designed, efforts are often made to include all the theatre's functions, including technical staff and management, in the same building. This, of course, has long been the rule in Europe, but it doesn't guarantee there that technicians will enjoy the special qualities and problems of theatre production. In fact, Leo Skodik, the longtime technical director of Berlin's prestigious state theatre, the Schiller, noted a change in attitude backstage, beginning in the 1960's. Before that time, he has said, even the least skilled of the stage carpenters would proudly boast to strangers: "I'm a member of the Schiller Theatre!" And, what was more important, he would work on Sundays if a production was falling behind in construction schedule. Now, however, younger technical people often complain about working on Sundays, even though the Schiller plays seven days a week, rotating a number of different productions daily. Skodik has reported their objections: "My wife works from Monday to Friday, and I want to spend Sunday with her and the kids."

That is of course one of the problems of the theatre, and not just for technical workers. Its hours of preparation and performance are not those of the ordinary world of work. Anyone who decides on a career in theatre, whether on stage, backstage, or out in front of the house, should be prepared for some irregularity in work schedule.

One compensation for the theatre craft worker, however, if he is really skilled and eager to work, is that he will be apt to work more steadily, and often at better pay, than the majority of Equity actors. If acting is what you really want to do, you shouldn't become a stage carpenter just because you will be more economically secure. There would always be that gnawing feeling that, even though you *are* working in the theatre, you didn't have the courage to do what you really dreamed of doing. If, however, you know your talents lie in the technical or craft areas of theatre, there should be no problem of artistic frustration when you choose and train for the technical theatre career you believe you are qualified to pursue. If all goes well, you will be making a valuable contribution in congenial surroundings, working with artists and craftsmen who appreciate your contribution and who, generally, make it a real pleasure to call colleagues, even friends.

WORKING BEHIND THE SCENES

Actually, some very important technical work is done not *behind* the scenes, but well out in front of them. In most Broadway theatres, for instance, the follow-spot operators are confined in a tiny, hot booth constructed as an afterthought in the back of the balcony. As has been noted, most of these theatres were designed not for technical efficiency, but to cram as many seats as possible into the theatre. They were also designed at a time when many of the new, sophisticated stage-lighting instruments and techniques were unknown or considered too costly.

As a result, directors and designers who want to have effective control over changes in scenery, lighting, and sound often do not want it monitored from the wings of the stage, but from out front, where the technicians can really see the production in action as the audience does. Since there is usually no provision on Broadway for a control booth, sections of seats have to be taken over to make improvised control positions. If a lighting or sound technician has problems about having strangers watch him at work, he had better avoid these Broadway theatres. New theatres are customarily designed with rear-auditorium control booths, so you don't have to suffer stage fright while dimming the lights.

There are two major areas of production activity for theatre technicians and craftsmen. One is obviously that which involves the actual running of a show in performance. Not all these jobs require a high degree of skill or training, but even moving a chair on a stage—especially during a blackout—is not as simple as it might seem. The other important area is that concerned with preparing, building a production. There is also a third area of activity that may not be so interesting or exciting but is basic: that is maintaining the theatre building, its machinery, and equipment. In college and community theatres, and often in regional nonprofit theatres, the technical staffs take care of all three areas. Some may be limited to specific jobs by government or union regulation. If they are responsible for keeping the building in good condition, for instance, they may not be asked or permitted to work on set construction.

In some regional situations, technicians who run the shows are not required to work on preproduction technical jobs. In most, however, they have to contribute as much of their skill and time as possible on whatever jobs need to be done to make the season successful. In the commercial theatre, including touring companies, there is usually a clear division between the technical people who build the shows, those who run them, and those who maintain the theatre buildings. That custom was originally dictated by the realities of the theatres' construction: the shops have to be elsewhere. Also, by the way in which the houses have long been rented to producers by theatre owners who are seldom producers themselves: the production staff has to be different from the owner's theatre staff, even though his group is usually skeletal.

To review the various craft and technical jobs available, it may be useful to look first at those mainly involved in building productions. This will be followed by a consideration of the range of skills needed for the running of a show.

Building a Show

In a theatre that has its own technical staff for producing shows, there may be some organizational differences from similar theatres elsewhere. If a theatre ensemble has two—or even three—stages, the staff may well be larger than that for a single-stage company. It is also likely to have more subdivisions in various departments. Some technical functions in building a show, however, may not be carried out by staff members because they are needed too seldom to justify hiring a full-time expert. Or the skills are so specialized that there are not enough trained workers for each theatre to have its own expert.

With the Broadway theatre, of course, and with some commercial play and musical seasons elsewhere in the U.S., almost all the construction work must be done outside the theatre where the show will be produced. In New York, this means the scenery is often built by commercial studios such as Metro or Atlas. Costumes may be constructed in special workshops such as that operated by Barbara Matera or Ray Diffen. A recent Broadway musical, for instance, listed the following credits for technical work done on the production *outside* the walls of the Majestic Theatre: scenery built by Metro Scenery Studios; scenery painted by Nolan Scenery Studios; automation by Feller Precision; costumes executed by Barbara Matera; men's tailoring by George Deutsch; hats by Woody Shelp; wigs by Bob Kelly Wig Creation; sound equipment by Masque Sound and Recording; electrical equipment by Four Star Stage Lighting; draperies by I. Weiss and Sons; special projection systems by Bran Ferren—and *animals* by Animal Actors, Inc.

What this means to those of you who are serious about having a career in technical theatre is that there are a number of skilled, well-paid jobs available with firms that serve the producing theatre. Some skills can be practiced either in a theatre shop complex or in a commercial shop apart from a theatre. Others are often based entirely outside a producing theatre. In the list above, some of the firms actually built or created the items with which they are credited. Others merely rented them to the theatre company. Organizing and operating an enterprise that rents sound or lighting equipment to theatres may not sound glamorous, but it's essential and also profitable. There also have to be those technical experts who develop new kinds of theatre machinery, materials, systems, equipment, and processes. Such talents are welcome with the major manufacturers of theatre equipment. A good theatre architect will find a market for his skill. Not least important in the world of theatre technology are those men and women who help producers, directors, designers, and technical directors to learn about new materials and methods. Sometimes they are called consultants; sometimes they are called sales managers. To some people, being a salesman might seem to require no special training or skill. That is not the case with theatre equipment, materials, and processes. The sales representatives have to know the capabilities of the things they are selling. Often, if something goes wrong or is used incorrectly, they have to help correct the situation.

So there is room for many kinds of skills and interests in serving the theatre. An excellent way to keep informed of what is being done in theatre techniques and production is to read *Theatre Crafts* magazine and join the U.S. Institute of Theatre Technology.

No matter how democratic or "collective" a theatre acting company may be, there has to be an effective organizational system backstage and in commercial shops. There must be foremen or supervisors to determine what must be done, how and when it must be done, and by whom and with what. In a producing theatre, such as San Francisco's A.C.T. or Minneapolis's Guthrie, all the backstage work is supervised by one man. This is the technical director, or TD. All of the craft operations in the workshops are overseen by him, but they are under the direct supervision of experts in each of the crafts—master technicians and very effective managers.

Some of the technical jobs backstage require professional apprenticeships. Union regulations spell out what qualifications and training you must have in order to work in the commercial theatre. In some cases, union membership is so limited—to protect the limited number of jobs available—that it is almost impossible to be admitted no matter how skilled and well trained you may be. In community theatre, however, rules are seldom so rigid. There, you can learn a lot about the technical skill you wish to pursue while actually doing it. But, working in an amateur situation, you may lack the opportunity to learn from the professional background and experience of an older theatre technician.

Even in high school, though, you can learn something about technical theatre by working on shows. If you are really interested in lighting, costume building, or scene painting, you shouldn't limit yourself to school productions. Community and church theatre groups will also be glad to have your willing hands to help. In some cases, they may have equipment or problems that will give you more of a challenge than you can get on a high school production. A few high schools now have special courses in theatre production.

Majoring in theatre in college, especially one that is well known as a center of theatre study, is the best way for young people to find their way into the crafts and jobs they would most like to practice. Usually, you will be exposed to all aspects of theatre, including its history, when you are an undergraduate. If your obvious interests and talents lie in technical areas, instructors will help you begin to specialize. The big advantage of working in a college drama department, as opposed, for instance, to being taken on as an apprentice in a commercial costume shop, is that you have the chance to explore, to try out different kinds of technical jobs, to see what you like best and what you can do best. You often can learn—and make a living at—more than one skill.

At the graduate level, a number of noted drama schools provide a high level of technical training in various theatre specialties. Usually, the professors are themselves well-known theatre technicians. Not only will they be offering the basics you need for your projected profession, but they will also be able to tell you about the latest equipment and procedures. Because of their reputations and their connections in the professional theatre, they can help you find a good job. Some graduate programs even require a semester or two of internship with a producing regional theatre. Students have frequently been hired by the theatres in which they were interns, so well have they learned their lessons, done their work, and fitted into the theatre family.

Working in summer stock or in summer outdoor drama and Shakespeare festivals can also provide invaluable training experience in stagecraft and theatre technology. Competition for such jobs is often stiff. Some theatres offer much better learning experiences than others, so you should choose carefully and then present your qualifications in the most effective manner, stressing your dedication and enthusiasm, so that the theatre will want you to work with its ensemble.

To give you an idea of the various preproduction technical skills needed in most theatres, it may be helpful to list the major categories. It should be remembered, however, that in some small theatres, one person may be in charge of costume construction, materials purchasing, wigmaking, footwear, makeup, and wardrobe management during production. Depending on the size of the theatre and its programs, you may have to do many jobs—before, during, and after production—or you may have one specific job. Here are some possible technical positions:

Technical Director. The TD is responsible for all the technical work in the production. The larger the operation, the more people under the direction of the TD. The TD is responsible for supervising design, construction, lighting, setting up, shifting, and striking. In smaller theatres, the TD may act as the lighting designer, set designer, or stage manager. A TD must know the precise specifications and measurements of the theatre or complex in which the show is produced.

Coordinator/Scheduler. Larger theatres and performing arts complexes require complicated coordinating and scheduling. Rehearsals, performances, workshops, and everything else must be cleared by the coordinator to avoid time-consuming conflicts. The coordinator/scheduler in an opera company is especially busy, with hundreds of people and spaces. Imagine dealing with space, singers, conductors, extras, musicians, technical personnel, and more. It can be a full-time balancing act.

Facilities Manager. Performing arts complexes are growing larger and require a staff completely separate from the production staff. However, management of the facilities must still be carried out in a manner that keeps foremost the needs of the artists and audiences. The facilities manager supervises maintenance, security, heating, and air conditioning. Snack bars and concessions may also be under his control. The comfort of the audience and performers can be critical to the success of a performing arts organization.

Scene Shop Foreman. The scene shop foreman controls the workshop where sets are constructed with a variety of materials. The foreman must know the tools and techniques necessary to advise and supervise the scene shop workers. The foreman coordinates closely with the technical director as well as the director and producer.

Draftsman. The theatrical draftsman provides detailed drawings of complex set designs and theatrical machinery. This work must meet the exacting specifications of the designers and the theatre space.

Carpenter. Working primarily in the scene shop, the carpenters create the sets and devices used in the production. Theatrical carpenters require special skills and use specialized materials. They are usually skilled in cabinetmaking and are often called upon to create sets that are historically accurate. This could involve building only the front of a Louis XIV cabinet, which would appear to be an entire piece of furniture to the audience. Theatrical carpenters learn the art of making a locale on stage appear real when it may only be made of cloth and wood.

Metalworker. Metalworkers should be good sculptors as well. Metalworkers are involved in building complicated sets. In addition to metalwork, they must be familiar with handling plastic, fiberglass, and styrofoam.

Scenic Artist. Scenic artists paint the sets after the designs are prepared by the set designer and director. While the show is being planned, the scenic artist may be asked to create conceptual drawings along with the set designer. Many renderings may be produced before the design is actually chosen. Scenic artists should be able to work in black and white as well as color. They are called upon to create accurate models of proposed designs and should possess some drafting skills. The scenic artist creates the sets and artwork for the actual production.

Prop Shop Foreman. Large theatres require an entire properties shop or even a warehouse in which to create and store properties. If you are a collector, you may enjoy the responsibility for acquiring and keeping track of the hundreds of props needed for a theatrical production. The prop shop foreman works with the director to choose or buy the props needed. The value of items in some prop shops runs into millions of dollars.

Artisan. Many dance, theatre, and opera companies employ professional artisans. Artisans are knowledgeable craftsmen who are able to manufacture properties that are historically accurate.

Costume Shop Foreman/Wardrobe Chiefs and Assistants. The costume shop foreman inventories and controls the expensive costume collections. The costume shop may have many employees, including seamstresses, wigmakers, and milliners who construct costumes according to the costume designer's specifications, under the foreman's supervision.

A difficult job for the costume shop foreman and the staff is "pulling" the costumes off the racks after months or years of storage and preparing them for use in a revival or altering them for a new production.

Pattern Drafters and Fabric cutters. Pattern drafters work in the costume shop. They are required to create the patterns for costumes from the costume designer's sketches or from a draped and pinned swatch of cloth. Cutting the fabric for theatrical costumes can be very tricky and requires a steady hand and a high degree of skill.

Tailor/Seamstress. Tailors and seamstresses must be ready to produce costumes that can be altered to fit a variety of actors. In case of deterioration, loss, or destruction of costumes, the tailor must be able to reproduce them exactly.

Milliner. Milliners must be able to build hats from raw materials. This is a skill that the costume shop foreman is often required to master. Milliners are also expert rebuilders. Hats may have to be historically accurate, or special headdresses may be needed, such as those used in the play *Equus:* framework horses' heads for actors to wear.

Shoemaker. Shoemakers are most commonly found in dance organizations. They build shoes as well as repair and maintain them. Shoemakers also purchase shoes for the company. Shoemakers who specialize in delicate ballet shoes are especially valued.

Wigmaker. Although most performing arts organizations purchase ready-made wigs, the larger opera companies, regional theatres, and Broadway shows use their own wigmakers. In addition to making wigs out of synthetic or natural hairs, the wigmaker may also be asked to create wigs out of other materials for special effects and unusual styles.

Makeup Expert. A necessity in all theatre is the makeup expert or artist. Actors with many years of experience often become expert in applying their own makeup, but the makeup specialist has studied many years in college and on the job to create a Dracula or a Wizard. The makeup expert may be asked to create effects and then teach the actors to apply the makeup themselves. In casts that have a chorus line, the makeup expert must help to assure uniformity in the application of makeup.

Fabric Buyer. Fabric buyers are experts in the fabric market. They make purchases and build up inventories for the costume shops by watching for special buys. The fabric buyer can save an organization many thousands of dollars.

Fabric Dyer. In theatre some fabrics and backdrops are used repeatedly. A certain costume may be right for a show, but the color may be wrong. Fabrics are dyed repeatedly. This specialization is used in the costume shop, but the dyer has a special dye room with the huge vats and equipment necessary to do the job.

Lighting Engineer and Assistants. The more complicated the equipment, the more demand there is for the lighting engineer. Often the lighting engineer is a fully licensed electrician. He or she may have a specialized electrical background as well as performing arts training. A beginning in lighting skills can be gained in high school productions, learning to install the gel sheets and focus the lights. The technical knowledge required can be obtained in college.

Sound Engineer and Assistants. As in lighting, this skill can be developed in high school, working the tape or record decks or setting up the microphones. But, increasingly, more extensive knowledge is needed to run sound systems that can be as complicated as those used in rock concerts. Mixing, recording, and putting sounds together with live performances requires a delicate ear and a fine touch.

Wardrobe Manager. Large costume collections in larger companies require management. The wardrobe manager also builds the costume inventory by making special buys, sometimes purchasing wardrobes of shows that have closed or of other theatres or organizations that have gone out of business. The wardrobe manager inventories, controls, and helps to maintain the costume collection.

Depending on the size and complexity of a theatre's program, of course, there may be more than one assistant in various technical areas. Sometimes, owing to the special talents of a theatre craftsman, a job title may be created to label appropriately the specialty he practices. A very few, for instance, have developed the skills needed to make projection slides for special optical effects in theatre productions. Some technicians, working for both costume and prop shops, are expert in the use of hot glue or other materials and processes that make new visual effects possible on stage.

Major European theatres customarily employ many more technicians than do American theatres. The budgets are much larger; so are the programs of production and the inventories of supplies and equipment that must be maintained. It is not unusual for a European theatre to have a complete metalworking shop, for example. This is a rarity in the United States, where complicated metalwork is often subcontracted outside the theatre—or avoided. Simpler metalwork, whether it involves the cutting of sheet metal, the bending of reinforcement rods, or the welding of metal braces, is done by the technicians who customarily work with wood and fabric.

It is also common in large European theatres to have separate shops for cabinetmaking—furniture is frequently designed specially for a new production instead of being bought or rented—and for sculpting. All kinds of prop statuary and architectural elements such as pillars, friezes, and moldings are made in the sculpture shop. Sometimes the artists work in plaster, sometimes celastic, sometimes in real wood. Or they may use hot-knives to carve blocks of styrofoam. Again, in America, someone on the prop or scenic construction staff would usually do this work, or it would be contracted from an outside firm. Mixing paints and dyes is another specialist job in Europe, unlike America. Some theatres have their own costume cleaning plants.

Styles and tastes in production design, of course, have a very real bearing on what skills may be in demand backstage and how many technicians may be needed. At times, a theatre's artistic director and its designers may favor projections instead of much solidly built scenery. When that is the case, electricians, artists, and photographers have more chances for work than do carpenters. Because the idea of handsomely subsidized theatre is relatively new to Americans, most theatres cannot afford the technicians they would like to have, not to mention the work space, the materials, and the machinery. But that may well come in the future, and you can be ready to take part in that technical development. If you master a language such as German, you could also gain valuable experience interning or working in a European theatre that has impressively equipped and staffed technical shops (especially if you don't mind working backstage on Sundays now and then).

As the construction and rehearsal of a production moves forward, the artistic staff works closely with the technical staff to make sure that everything will function effectively. The theatre's management staff is also busily at work to ensure that the seats are filled for the production, insofar as advertising and ticket-sales promotions can do this. On the artistic side, the director and the various designers usually have assistants who coordinate with the tech departments. This is vital in commercial Broadway theatre, where rehearsals may be taking place in Greenwich Village while the projected theatre is on 45th Street and the scene-construction shops are in Long Island City. Much more coordination is required than in a regional theatre where everyone is working under one roof.

"Assistant" has an official sound to it, and often assistants have a lot of responsibility, leading in time to important jobs as designers and supervisors. You shouldn't be too disappointed, however, if you are hired as an assistant and find that what you really are is a "Go-

For." Sometimes it's spelled "Gopher," but it means: "Go for a cuppa coffee, will ya?" "Get me a paper and pencil, *right now!*" "Go tell that idiot electrician to get that light adjusted!"

Running a Show

The technical staff that actually runs a show in performance is usually different, in professional theatre, from those who built it. But the smaller and poorer the theatre, the more doubling and tripling of jobs there will be. The stage manager, who is the director's representative once the show opens, is responsible for overseeing everything that goes on backstage, on stage, and some things out front. To gain this mastery, he works with both producer and director very closely from the first days of rehearsal. Other crew members will come into the production only at those stages where their skills or efforts are needed. When the sets are finished and the costumes are on the dressing-room racks, the full complement of stagehands, dressers, and others will be needed to complete rehearsals and get the show running smoothly. The lighting technician or engineer and his staff will be hanging and focusing lighting instruments to correspond to the light-plots devised by the lighting designer, often with the designer himself in close attendance. A technical rehearsal helps the tech staffs to make sure that everything is working right: no doors will fall off their hinges as Al Pacino makes his grand entry as Tartuffe. The follow-spot on Barbra Streisand won't suddenly burn out. Carol Burnett's wig won't be blown off by the wind machine. The beauty of Anne Bancroft's pink silk evening gown won't be ruined because someone put green gels into the Fresnel lighting instruments.

Skilled technical people take a great pride—an artist's pride—in making a show run as brilliantly and as effortlessly as possible. Of course some shows, especially musicals, require a lot of effort, with difficult scene changes or complicated and massive changes of costumes from scene to scene. But the point for the tech people is to plan and rehearse the operation of a production so well that the audience thinks it is done virtually without effort. If changes that the audience can see—and the tension it can sense behind the scenes—suggest too much hard work, the viewers' enjoyment may be spoiled.

Even though it has been noted that being on a tech crew is a good way to avoid the terrors of stage fright, crew chiefs who have to be out front manning lighting and sound control boards must be able to do their jobs without distracting audience attention. Stagehands who have to be seen on stage shifting flats or removing or regrouping furniture must have enough presence to do their jobs swiftly, carefully, and impersonally. If the audience, in a good humor, applauds them, they should know how to react—smile or ignore it.

Here are some of the kinds of technical workers needed to run a production.

Stage Manager. The stage manager, who was mentioned in Chapter I, is in full charge of the production after the director leaves, usually after the dress rehearsal. During the production the stage manager uses the prompt book developed during rehearsals to call all the sound, light, special effects, and other cues. The stage manager may hold rehearsals during the run of the show to assure that it remains as directed originally. The stage manager may also rehearse new members of the cast as others leave.

Production Stage Manager. On Broadway and in larger companies, the production stage manager starts with the show from its conception and works with the producer and director. The production stage manager mainly oversees the technical aspects. Like the technical director, the production stage manager is responsible for set construction, lighting, and sound. If the show is very technically oriented, he will stay through the run and help the stage manager to supervise the strike.

Master Carpenter. The master carpenter becomes responsible for the handling and repair of all the scenery used during the production. Along with the stage manager, the master carpenter supervises the set-ins, scene changes, the stage crew, and the eventual striking of the set.

Stagehand. The stagehands set the stage, move scenery during shifts, handle props, and strike the set. In smaller theatres or regional theatres, stagehands may double as carpenters and work in the scene shop between productions to build sets.

Flyman. The flyman is the stagehand who handles the ropes that "fly" the scenery. Usually, only the flyman (or woman) is permitted to touch the ropes that hold scenery and other flown objects.

Property Master. The property master has to preset all the props used in the production. The responsibilities include inventory of the items used. The prop master is in charge of dress props, set props, and the personal props carried by the actors.

Master Electrician. Master electricians and others working on lights are sometimes called "juicers." The master electrician is responsible for the electrical set-in, hanging, wiring, and focusing of the lights. The electrician also supervises the running of the lights during the show and, of course, participates in the strike of the lights and wiring.

Follow-spot Operator. Usually employed in musicals or variety shows, the follow-spot operator uses a single spotlight to focus on and highlight a specific performer. This is more difficult than it looks, especially during a dance number.

Projectionist. Projectionists are being utilized increasingly in American theatre productions where a clever projection can take the place of expensive scenery. Projectionists are familiar with various types of equipment.

Wardrobe Master/Mistress. In productions requiring many costumes and costume changes, the wardrobe master/mistress plays an important role. He or she must be sure that the costumes are laid out in the proper order for costume changes and must supervise the dressers and seamstresses. He or she is also responsible for cleaning and maintaining the costumes while they are in use and returning them with as little damage as possible to the costume shop or costume rental house.

Dresser. The dresser works under the supervision of the wardrobe master/mistress. In shows requiring many costume changes, the dresser helps to accomplish the changes in as little time as possible. Often, stars or leading characters have a special dresser assigned to them.

Makeup Expert. Cast members are expected to apply their own makeup when the director and the makeup artist have agreed on its design. Sometimes, difficult makeups or masks require continued help of the makeup expert. In a large cast, the makeup expert helps the cast to have a uniform look.

Hair Stylist. As with makeup, the cast members are responsible for their own hair styles, but when special styling or certain wigs are used, a hair stylist works with the actors. Many stars have personal hair stylists who work with them on every show.

Sound Technician. During the production the sound technician may also be called the sound master. He runs all the sound cues as called by the stage manager and is responsible for the sound system for the run of the show. In addition to the systems used out front, the sound technician installs and operates an intercom system so that the production staff can communicate during the running of the show.

Stage Engineer. On Broadway and in other large theatres, a stage engineer works with the production staff. This licensed engineer supervises all safety systems and makes sure that the production staff uses the theatre equipment properly. The stage engineer, who is usually employed by the theatre owners, sees that the heating, air-conditioning, and other comfort systems are operating properly.

Stage Doorman. The stage doorman does more than the name implies. Aside from being responsible for the stage door, he is also in charge of backstage security. The stage doorman (or woman) makes sure that only the cast and staff enter the backstage area. He keeps theatre and production property, and sometimes personal valuables, under lock and key.

Although this book doesn't deal with careers in cinema or radio/TV broadcasting, many of the technical skills mentioned above are also in great demand in those performance media. Building sets for a TV show requires much the same talent and training needed to construct a Broadway production. Film and TV may occasionally call for sets with more detail and realism—with the camera lens often up so close—than the stage, but really professional carpenters and scenic artists are equally capable of working for all the performing arts. The same is true of costuming, makeup, wigmaking, and similar crafts.

The truth is that the best designers and craftsmen work where the work is. If the commercial theatre is having a poor season, as is sometimes the case, technicians who are not already on the annual payroll of a theatre company, a commercial theatre workshop, or a theatre supply and equipment house will often find work in film and TV production, especially if they are located in or move to production centers such as New York and Los Angeles. What is more, this work is challenging and well paid. Obviously, both films and television, because of the technology through which performances are recorded on film or on videotape or transmitted live on TV, require some technical skills that are not used in the theatre. That means there are even more job categories in those two forms of production, not covered in this book. But whether you wish to work in living theatre exclusively or in all performance forms or media, if you have some new specialty, some hitherto unused technique or talent, you can make a place for yourself as a valued technician or artist. Sometimes, it is difficult to decide whether to call some theatre craftsmen "artists" or "artisans." A designer may have created the visual image of a costume, but a tailor, a draper, a cutter all may contribute creative touches to the finished costume.

That is why famous designers and directors so often ask to have their productions built by specific firms, to have special technicians work with them in bringing their dream of a production to vibrant life on stage.

CHAPTER V

Your Career in Performing Arts Management

No records have survived of the theatre's first beginnings. But there are records of ritual religious drama in ancient Egypt. A lot of information has survived about the classic Greek theatre. One thing these records make clear is that some form of performance management was essential.

Obviously, no planning, no publicity, no concern for audience admission and seating were necessary if a Greek shepherd, sitting on a hillside, decided he wanted to play his flute. It was quite a different matter, however, when the city-state of Athens was preparing for its annual City Dionysia in the Theatre of Dionysus at the foot of the Acropolis. Three major writers of tragedy would compete, each with four new plays. Comic playwrights would also contest with each other for the honor of being judged best. Ten choruses of fifty performers each would vie with each other in performing a danced, chanted ode to the god Dionysus. Not only would every citizen of Athens be entitled to a seat—with subsidies for the poorest if they couldn't afford the low admission price—but foreign merchants and dignitaries would be honored guests. This festival of dancing, singing, and acting was not only the central part of a religious observance and a major public entertainment, but it was also an effective means of displaying the culture and wealth of Athens. Thus, nothing could be left to chance. Everything had to run smoothly, considering the numbers of performers and spectators involved. Athens' leaders wanted to ensure that the festival would not only run smoothly, but brilliantly as well.

Whether dance, drama, or musical performances have been the care of the state, the church, or private individuals and ensembles, throughout recorded history they have always had to have various arts management services in order to prosper, or even to survive. This has been especially important for performance groups that were not supported by wealthy patrons or the government. Often it was the head of the troupe who was responsible for the major management decisions, aided in the details by various members of the ensemble. In the late 18th and the 19th centuries, both in England and America, this role was filled by the actor-manager.

As leading actor of his company, he chose the ensemble and held it together. He selected the plays, assigned the parts, decided where and when the company would play. If his vanity was greater than his common sense, the company might find itself in trouble. He might decide to do plays the audiences wouldn't like just because a certain role appealed to him. He might deny talented young performers a fair chance, fearing that they could eclipse him. He might use up whatever profits the company was making to mount a new production in too expensive a manner.

Of course the best actor-managers did not let their egos get in the way of good management. If unwise decisions and careless spending were to bankrupt the troupe, how would they be able to practice their art? Still, it was asking a lot for a major performer to give his best on stage eight times a week and also attend to complicated details of planning, rehearsing, and bookkeeping—and, often, touring. In the commercial theatre, both in America and abroad, these actor-managers were eventually replaced by theatre manager-owners who were primarily businessmen.

In the early decades of this century, most New York theatres were owned or controlled by the Shubert brothers. They had replaced an earlier monopoly, often called the Syndicate. Around the U.S., the Shuberts also bought up theatres to be sure that their touring attractions would have plenty of stages for performances. In some cases, they didn't own the theatres but made agreements with the owners that only Shubert shows would be booked. They were themselves prolific producers, and they also worked with other producers who had to play the Shubert houses.

You can guess that artistic excellence was not the first concern of men who saw the theatre as a means of making a profit. Quite a big profit, as things turned out. (Even today, in Manhattan some seventeen theatres are still controlled by the Shubert interests.) Where profit is a prime concern, clearly a number of elements that are important to creating a really fine musical, dance, or dramatic production are apt to be slighted or even ignored.

Thus, there is an interesting contrast between the two types of managers. One, the actor-manager, might be more financially careless to serve what he saw as his art. The other, the businessman, could be a financial fanatic to the disservice of performing arts. You cannot create the impression of a lavish spectacle on stage if you are pinching pennies and cutting corners. You will not have a memorable production if you hire unknown actors or dancers or singers because you don't want to meet the fees of talented artists.

Fortunately, in today's drama, dance, and music theatres a new kind of manager is emerging. Stephen Langley, in his vital book *Theatre Management in America,* calls this new talent the "Third-Century Manager." The 18th and 19th centuries had their distinctive managers; now the 20th century has begun to develop a new breed, men and women who will be ready for the challenge to the performing arts in the 21st century—which isn't very far off!

It has often been said that the bottom line for the theatre businessman was always "the buck." For the actor-manager, it was his art or his ego, or both. For the new manager, however, the concerns are not that simple. Balancing the books is important, but if the theatre's work is not of good artistic quality, why make the effort? There must be artistic striving side by side with fiscal stability. In fact, astute observers of the American theatre scene, both in New York and around the nation, have noted that a number of artistically distinguished drama, dance, and opera ventures have failed because of mounting deficits that they could not manage to pay off. In many cases, it was clear that more careful budgeting of resources, combined with more effective publicity and ticket sales, plus more inventive methods of winning corporate and foundation support, would have saved the ensembles.

Marcella Cisney, a New York stage director and for a number of years the guiding spirit of the Professional Theatre Program in Ann Arbor, Michigan, was fond of pointing this out even when she was working as an artistic director. "We have enough geniuses in the theatre, brilliant artistic directors. What our theatre really needs is arts managers! People who know how to say "NO" to an artistic director who wants to use up the whole season's budget on one show. The one he is directing, of course."

Today, some performance groups are managed in that way. There is a gifted artistic director with all kinds of exciting plans for new plays, wonderful productions, remarkable actors, and innovative techniques. Opposite him is a well-trained business manager who keeps telling him: "It won't work"; "The theatre can't afford it"; "It's too complicated"; "The audience won't know the difference anyway." That is like the government's system of checks and balances, but it is often an awkward and even unpleasant way to create art.

The problem is that such arrangements can have too much of an adversary nature about them. Instead of working together for a common artistic aim, the artist and the businessman are fighting with each other, one ostensibly for art, the other for solvency. Of course, there are situations in which management responsibilities are somewhat evenly divided, artistic on one side, business on the other, and the results are admirable because the two people in charge like and respect each other. In the theatre, that is an ideal to be sought at all levels, but in the real world it doesn't always happen.

It comes down to the fact that things work better when only one person is in charge. The committee is not the perfect theatre manager. Someone has to be responsible for the final decision. But, in one well-known American regional theatre some years ago, the artistic director used up virtually all the company's reserves on a production in which he had become deeply involved. It was impressive enough and would surely attract audiences, but the ensemble was only in the middle of its season, with three more productions to be mounted and no more money in sight. The business manager curtailed some of the director's proposed expenditures on the play. The director stopped speaking to him in annoyance and anger. (He may also have realized that his partner was right about the financial problems.) After several weeks of silence, the director told his manager that they couldn't continue that way, not speaking. So he fired the manager, who had never refused to speak.

This also shows that the theatre is not always one big happy family. In 1965 a Rockefeller Panel on the Performing Arts formulated a very challenging description of an effective arts manager, one that is also quoted in Langley's comprehensive study of management principles and practices:

> . . . a person who is knowledgeable in the art with which he is concerned, an impresario, labor negotiator, diplomat, educator, publicity and public relations expert, politician, skilled businessman, a social sophisticate, a servant of the community, a tireless leader—becomingly humble before authority—a teacher, a tyrant, and a continuing student of the arts.

Although some of the phrasing makes it seem that the panel members were smiling a bit when they composed this list of excellences, it is basically a fairly accurate description of the talents a good performing arts manager should possess. Of course, few people have all of those qualities, but a potentially effective manager should have most of them. If he is lacking some, he can develop them with time and effort.

Performing arts management isn't just a matter of the right man at the top of the organizational pyramid. It is very important to have the right man also well supported by a highly skilled staff in the various areas of arts management. This can make an ensemble not merely survive, but also thrive. Selecting, building, training such a staff can be the responsibility of an able artistic director or managing director founding a new group. More often, in an established ensemble, an incoming director has to work with the structure and staff he finds. If things are not working well, he may make crucial changes in administrative goals and procedures. He may fire some of the staff, or he may help them to redirect their energies and attitudes more effectively. In a healthy arts organization, there is, however, a lot of give and take. If a new director is engaged, staff members should want to discuss with him the way things have been done in the past and possible new ways of working in the future. They may be able to show him that some new ideas are not going to work for the group. He may be able to open them up to new ways of building audiences or cutting costs that will be most welcome.

In a producing theatre complex, such as the Metropolitan Opera or the Arena Theatre in Washington, D.C., arts management may be seen as a third element of a trio, with artists and technicians as the other two essential elements. In the commercial theatre, where the producer and the theatre owner usually have separate organizations, many of the same management talents are also needed, though the procedures and goals are sometimes changed to meet the special demands of promoting Broadway shows and touring companies. In addition, a number of arts management jobs are available with firms that contract their services—such as publicity, audience surveys, and consultancy—to producers and artistic directors. Even performers may need to employ the abilities of some skilled people in the areas of personal publicity, career management, and financial advisement.

Nonprofit but thoroughly professional drama, dance, opera, and music ensembles have been a minor feature of American life. They are now on the increase, even though all kinds of costs in production are mounting. Great American symphony orchestras such as those in New York, Boston, Philadelphia, Chicago, and San Francisco have long, honored traditions. As do the Metropolitan Opera and the somewhat younger San Francisco Opera. More recent are such fine ensembles as the New York City Ballet and the City Opera. All over America, however, in Seattle, in Houston, new dance and music performance groups are springing up. In some cities the production season may be confined to only a few weekends or a month or two in fall and spring, but these are clearly beginnings in a nation that has long looked primarily to the commercial arts producers for its culture and entertainment. These are nonprofit groups dedicated to real artistic achievement. Supporting that requires a combination of state, corporate, and private subsidy, which has been largely unknown in America except for major art museums and symphonies.

Curiously, of the performing arts, only theatre has generally been assumed by the public to be able to make its own way financially. Most people accept the idea that serious arts, such as opera, symphony, chamber music, choruses, classical ballet, and modern dance, cannot expect to make a profit at the box office. They must be subsidized. For years, theatre has been viewed as a profit-making enterprise. It is still not unusual to hear someone who doesn't know much about theatre management say: "If it's any good, it's got to make money! If it's no good, it will fail!" What such a speaker really means by "good" is "popular." Of course the play or musical that appeals to the largest number of people will make the most money and be—by monetary standards—the best, the most successful. But box office receipts are not the most reliable measure of artistic truth and quality. A "crowd-pleaser" of a show must always make a number of artistic compromises in order to appeal to widely diverse audiences that may run into thousands and millions. But it's clear that some fine plays, ballets, and operas cannot hope to appeal to everyone.

More and more, that is being understood by people who love the theatre but who are not of it. Audiences who want to enjoy theatre of the very highest artistic achievement understand that such programs do not come out of the rough-and-tumble of the marketplace. That means that just as opera, serious instrumental music, and dance are not treated as commodities to be sold for profit, theatre in some of its aspects should also be viewed as a cultural resource, like fine museums, libraries, and parks.

No one is suggesting that the popular commercial theatre should be despised, ignored, or closed down. It fills an important social need as well. Indeed, it is today often renewed with plays and performers tested in nonprofit regional theatres. The one kind of theatre needs and feeds the other. What shouldn't be forgotten about the so-called commercial theatre is how many *millions* of dollars have been lost each season on failed shows. For every show that makes a handsome return to its investors, several others die after opening night with a loss of as much as one or two million dollars. That kind of investment is reckless gambling on a huge scale.

This means that management problems are major concerns for the performing arts, whether profit or nonprofit. It also means that good management people at all levels are just as important to the success of a dance troupe, an opera workshop, or a drama ensemble as the artists, though they are largely invisible to the public.

In the list of management jobs that follow, you will observe that some kinds of work have little relation to others. The talents and training that make a careful, methodical accountant may be of little use in the public relations department, where inventiveness, spontaneity, energy, enthusiasm, and personal charm are prime assets. And, though you can easily learn to be a methodical bookkeeper, charm and enthusiasm are not so readily teachable. The important thing to bear in mind, if you think performing arts management might be a good field for you to work in, is what you consider your real abilities and interests to be right now. Look for management positions that relate to your interests and talents. Even if you hate math, you might be able to force yourself to do well enough to become an accountant. But what would be the sense of that—even though it usually pays well—if it's work you really dislike all your life? Whereas if you like to write, to design, to chat on the phone, to meet people, to plan parties, you may have some very useful talents for the work of a public relations manager. There is a lot to be said for working in a career that you do very well and enjoy a great deal.

For those posts that involve management of large sums of money, high school commercial courses are a must, though everyone who works in the performing arts ought to master typing. College courses in economics, accountancy, and business methods can be invaluable, of course. You don't have to have a master's degree in Business Administration from Harvard or Stanford to be a producer or a general manager, but such training certainly won't hurt. More to the point, however, are specific courses and programs in arts management. Business administration courses, though dealing in basics, tend to prepare you for much broader management areas. There are a lot of rather special things you need to know about how the theatre and its performance forms actually work. These you won't learn in a business school. Some of them you will have to learn from painful on-the-job experience, but a great deal can be mastered through classes. When you are an undergraduate, general theatre training will be most helpful; you need to learn about forms, theatres, and performance practices. Some basic courses in economics and business will also be useful. At the graduate level, you should concentrate on management studies. This is a growing field, but as yet only a few colleges offer effective training. There are programs at the University of California in Los Angeles and, in New York, at New York University and Brooklyn College, for example. The Brooklyn

MFA program is directed by Stephen Langley, whose book *Theatre Management in America* is a complete course in itself.

Just as young performers and technicians learn by doing, so also do management interns. Even if you cannot enter a graduate management program, you may still be able to have a management career by taking special courses, carefully chosen from available evening college offerings, and by getting a job with a performing arts ensemble. With small groups, there may be no money to pay you. That shouldn't matter, since you will be partially paid by the experience you gain. Often, volunteers have done such a good job that they have virtually created a position for themselves. If the artistic director or the business manager find that they cannot get along without your abilities, they will find a way to pay you.

For those positions that require union membership—though not all ensembles work with union contracts—basic requirements in talent and training are set by the respective unions. Some have a stiff exam to admit only the best qualified and to keep out too much competition for the limited jobs. Minimum pay scales are also established, but outside New York there may be differences. Local unions often adjust their demands to the local situation. Of course, if you are really very good at your job, a producer or a manager may want to pay you well above the minimum to keep anyone else from hiring you away from him. In cases where the job is not covered by union protection, you will have to bargain with your potential employer to establish your duties, hours, and wages. Unless you are already very well known in your field, you may find that the producer is holding all the trump cards. That is why many theatre workers are pleased that they are represented in bargaining by unions. Sometimes the union leadership may make decisions that artists and craftsmen believe to be mistaken or harmful to the theatre, but, since the union is supposed to be a collective of equals, they certainly have the responsibility to correct wrongs from within their own unions. For the benefits, however, members have to pay a price. Union dues can be high; they can even be directly related to your earning power.

WORKING IN PERFORMING ARTS MANAGEMENT

Because the nonprofit "institutional" performing arts organizations are becoming so numerous and influential in American cultural life, it will be useful to survey the management jobs they make possible before considering positions in the commercial sector of the performing arts. One of these nonprofit groups is San Francisco's American Conservatory Theatre, or A.C.T. In 1979 it received a special Tony Award for its excellence as a professional regional theatre. At that time, its management structure included the following titles and functions:

General Director. Responsible for all artistic decisions and final say, after consultation, on all other major problems. The visible head of the theatre, its chief spokesman, and one of its most gifted stage directors.

Executive Producer. Responsible for overseeing all aspects of financial planning and funding, negotiates contracts, outside bookings.

Executive Director. Responsible for carrying out artistic decisions and assisting in decision-making, supervising plays in progress and special workshops. Also a stage director.

Development Director. Responsible for developing subsidy sources at the national level, as well as helping the company win an international identity.

Conservatory Director. Responsible for supervising professional training programs for ensemble members and students, taught by company members. Also a stage director.

Director of Artists and Repertory. Responsible for dramaturgic functions—play reading, adapting, and selection—as well as casting and scheduling company members in productions.

General Manager. Responsible, under the relevant directors above, for coordinating and carrying out decisions and policies.

Special Projects Director. Responsible for keeping management informed of city, county, and state legislation affecting arts subsidies, theatre production, business operation; concerned with fund-raising for company projects. (A large portion of the company's subsidy income is raised from grants and donations developed by The California Association for A.C.T., effectually a board of directors, with paid development/fund-raising staff and a number of support organizations staffed by theatre-loving volunteers.)

Business Manager. Responsible for ensuring that budgets are carefully worked out and followed, for supervising income and expenditures, and related fiscal duties, such as ensuring that union contract provisions are observed.

Bookkeeper. Responsible for maintaining the financial records.

Administrative Secretary. Responsible for secretarial duties.

Receptionists. Responsible for directing calls to appropriate personnel, giving information, and welcoming visitors.

Administrative Assistant. Responsible for helping where and as needed.

Management Intern. Graduate student of performing arts management, learning on the job.

Then there are the special management departments, answerable to the general administration and, through it, to the top-level managers:

Public Relations Staff:

Director of Press and Public Relations. Responsible for directing all relations with the news media, including issuing news releases and production-related photographs; arranging interviews and public appearances for theatre artists; conceiving and executing ideas to attract attention to the theatre and its productions; preparing the theatre programs; maintaining files of background information on the theatre and biographies of its personnel; keeping files on stories and reviews concerning theatre productions. This is a demanding job, for this is the person who helps give the theatre its public image and promotes its repertoire. The task is shared among the following co-workers: Press Representative, Administrative Assistant, Office Manager, Receptionist, Typist, Group and Student Sales Representative—which is an important aspect of public relations in building audiences, and Communications personnel.

Marketing Staff:

Marketing Director. Responsible, with consultation, for conceiving and developing promotional campaigns—including ads, TV spots, posters, slogans—to sell the theatre's season of plays to the public, working closely with the public relations people. He is assisted by a Production Manager, an Associate, an Art Director, a Designer, an Illustrator, an Artist, and an Administrative Assistant. (Some theatres have a house photographer to record productions and make photos for publicity and promotional purposes. This company engages a free-lance photographer.)

Subscriptions. This department, with a Manager, Assistant Manager, and staff, is responsible for making sure that subscribers not only are satisfied with the dates and seats they request, but also that they renew their subscriptions the following season—with the aid of public relations and marketing inducements. (Often, subscriptions, group sales, and other programs for selling tickets are grouped under the same department, but not here.)

Box Office Staff. Responsible for direct daily and advance ticket sales and for arranging changes in dates for subscribers who bring tickets in. This department is supervised by a Manager and an Assistant Manager, who must be very careful to keep a strict accounting of tickets and receipts, as well as to make sure that all the staff are friendly and courteous to the public.

Front of House Staff. Just as there has to be a tech crew backstage to run the show, so must there be a courteous, professional staff out front to make sure the theatre audience is welcomed and seated with ease and comfort. In charge is an Associate Manager, aided by two Doormen and a group of Ushers. (In some nonprofit theatres, public relations is served by allowing students to usher in return for a chance to see the production. In others, the ushers must belong to the union.) The lobby, lounges, and auditorium are also kept clean and in good condition by a custodial staff.

Some institutional theatres, whether dedicated to drama, dance, or opera, have an Educational Activities Director or a Schools Coordinator, whose work is often varied but usually centers on education-related events that bring members of the theatre family together with teachers and students. These can include class visits by actors, providing study guides and planning discussion groups, backstage tours and dressing-room visits, and even preparing radio and TV broadcasts to familiarize members of the community with the work of the group and the backgrounds of works being produced. Such programs are not only educational and often fun, but they also serve as promotion, winning new audience members for the theatre.

The A.C.T., however, makes education as important an activity as play production, through its remarkable conservatory. In its formative years, the A.C.T. found that treating its acting company as ongoing students who also could teach theatre skills made it possible to pay them through scholarships and grants. Today, company members are still learning skills from each other, and they also pass them on to teen-age students. (Second- and third-year students have the opportunity to work in professional productions of the A.C.T.) The conservatory officers include a Director, a Dean, an Assistant Conservatory Director, a Provost and Registrar, and an Assistant to the Registrar. The staff of Trainers is drawn from the acting ensemble.

Most nonprofit professional performance groups have a Board of Directors or a Board of Trustees. These positions are usually nonsalaried; a board may meet as seldom as once a year. Its function is to set general policies for the ensemble. If a new artistic director—or general manager, or general director, or executive director: the titles often mean the same—must be chosen, that is the responsibility of the board. If there are severe problems in the ensemble that the artistic director cannot himself solve, the board may be asked to help resolve them. Membership on some boards is appointive; on some, elective; on some, voluntary. Usually new members are invited to join by the board chairman and older members. This is not a career post in the theatre. Board membership frequently goes to people of wealth and influence in the community who can make sure that the company will have the financial security and public goodwill it needs to succeed. A well-stocked checking account is a good recommendation for board membership. Some community figures are not necessarily wealthy, but their positions as editors, churchmen, teachers, lawyers, politicians, or union leaders make them valued friends of the ensemble. (Performance groups often also have a Board of Advisors who are not expected to make up deficits but instead to give wise professional advice without charging consultant's fees.)

Some ensembles, especially dance troupes, have benefited from the generosity of just one person or a very small group of rich patrons. That can be a hazard: the patrons may eventually run out of money—or enthusiasm, as was the case twice with the Harkness Ballet. Since boards usually cannot devote themselves to the details of procuring grants and subsidies, many ensembles employ a fund-raiser, either full- or part-time.

Each performance group differs slightly or greatly in its administrative structure, depending on the kind of work it does, its size, its season, its audiences, and other significant variables. As a contrast to the A.C.T.'s roster, here is a brief listing of the Metropolitan Opera's range of jobs in 1979, under the three-headed leadership of James Levine (Music Director), John Dexter (Director of Production), and Anthony Bliss (Executive Director):

Artistic Administration. Artistic Administration Director, two Artistic Administrators, two Assistant Administrators, and one Assistant. Also of major importance to the Met, especially on tour, is its Company Manager and Musical Secretary, aided by an Assistant Musical Secretary. Not only does the Met have to decide which singers are good enough to sing on its stage, it also has to contract them—frequently for specific operas—several years in advance. Because many also sing on other world stages, their rehearsal and performance schedules must be carefully worked out. "Covers" or replacements must also be scheduled in case an artist suddenly is taken ill. Also listed under artistic administration are a Rehearsal Assistant, a Librarian, an Assistant Librarian, and a Staff Diction Coach, but this gives no idea of the numbers of people actually involved in the artistic side of opera rehearsal and performance.

Production Administration. A Technical Director, an Assistant Technical Director, a Production Coordinator, and an Administrative Assistant to the Director of Production help supervise the activities of the various theatre crafts, organized at the Met into three sectors: Design, Stage Management, and Stage and Shop Operations.

Business. Business Director, Assistant Business Director, Television Consultant to coordinate the details of live broadcasts or taping, Assistants.

Finance. Finance Director, Budget Director, Comptroller, Assistant Comptroller, Data Processing Manager, Budget Analyst, Senior Accountant, Cashier, Payroll Manager, Administrative Assistant. With annual budgets of $40 to $50 million, the Met needs these experts very much.

Development and Public Affairs. Director, Associate Director, Annual Giving Director, Patron Services Coordinator, Office Administrator, Research Assistant. The Met is very considerate of its generous patrons; it's also on the lookout for new donors as well.

Press and Public Relations. Director, Press Representative, Associate Press Representative, Assistant, Official Photographer, Assistant, Archivist, Assistant. Always courteous and helpful, the Met's press people win excellent publicity and goodwill for the ensemble.

Marketing. Director, Assistant Marketing Director, Ticket Services Manager, Subscription Coordinator, Mail Order Supervisor, Special Services Supervisor, Telephone Sales Supervisor, Assistant, Group Sales Supervisor, Promotion Manager, Assistant, Box Office Manager, Head Treasurer, Assistant, Opera Shop Manager, Libretto Supervisor. Most of these people are responsible for ensuring that the Met plays to sold-out houses. The last two sell you your opera souvenirs and texts.

House Management. House Manager, Associate House Manager, three Assistants, Chief Usher, Medical Director, Assistant Medical Director, Company Nurse, Stage Door Receptionist, Chief Engineer, Head Cleaning Lady, Head Porter. These are, of course, the chiefs; in a theatre as large as the Met, they supervise a lot of "Indians." Nor does the Met's printed administrative roster list those who provide dinners, snacks, and beverages in the Met's bars and restaurants.

The Met has a special Tour Director and Consultant, as well as a Presentations Director, who books troupes such as the Stuttgart Ballet into the house when the Met in on tour or holiday. There also are no less than seventeen Executive Secretaries to assist the major administrative officers of the Met. Considering the scores of soloists, choristers, dancers, supers, musicans, shop artisans, and stagehands it has to employ, schedule, supervise, and pay, it should be clear that a performance ensemble like the Met would dissolve in chaos and bankruptcy without its large, extremely well-organized administrative staff.

Of course, there's no guarantee that there will be a place open for you at the Metropolitan Opera, but it's well worth a try. It's not only an exciting place to work—even a secretary can watch a dress rehearsal now and then, not to mention chatting with a noted tenor at her desk—but it is also a beautiful, luxuriously equipped theatre in all its areas. But if you don't make it to the Met, or even to New York City, you may be able to learn a lot more about performing arts administration working with a small ensemble with an anemic budget. You might find yourself Director of Publicity, Marketing, Development, Finance, and the coffee-maker.

So the nonprofit professional theatre can offer you all sorts of challenges and possibilities in management. College theatres also have positions for good managers. Sometimes you will be expected to meet the academic requirements for faculty membership and to do some teaching as well, but in a number of schools your management training and experience will be sufficient qualification. Usage demands on college theatres can be hectic and astonishingly varied, but the salaries are generally good and regular, which cannot always be said of some nonprofit ensembles, which may expect you to raise your own salary and everyone else's as well.

To look now at the special administrative problems of the commercial theatre, it is necessary to distinguish three areas of administrative control. Unless the Shubert Organization is itself acting as the producer of a play or musical, it is more often functioning on Broadway as a theatre owner. The theatre owner, whether it be an individual or a corporation, must have a staff to operate the theatre for the production that is the tenant. When the New Apollo, reclaimed from years of use as a cinema, reopened, its Playbill listed the staff as: President, Vice President, Vice President/General Manager, Comptroller, Treasurer, House Manager, Carpenter, Electrician, Property Man, Director of Plant Operations, and Architect. Some of these jobs deal with stage production and theatre maintenance. (Some theatre owners contract outside firms to clean and maintain their theatres. Those, like the Shuberts and the Nederlanders, who own or control a number of theatres are able to employ larger staffs and can use certain personnel to attend to the needs of more than one theatre.)

Effective financial management is of major concern to the theatre owner. Although he is usually only renting performance space to a production, its success is important to him. On Broadway he doesn't rent the theatre on a "four wall" basis; instead, he collects a guaranteed weekly fee plus a percentage of the box office income above that guarantee. The better a show does at the box office, the more money he makes. If a show is doing poorly, he might like to see it closed to leave his theatre free for a new production that could make more money for him. He is sometimes helped in this by the fact that he, not the play's producers, contracts the treasurers and ticket sellers who take care of box office and mail-order sales. Obviously, the man who sells the tickets can, by being helpful or obstructive, have a real effect on sales.

Hiring the doormen, the ushering staff, and maintenance personnel is the theatre owner's responsibility, and he also contracts the house manager. On Broadway each theatre has an agreement with the International Alliance of Theatrical Stage Employees (IATSE) regarding the minimum number of crewmen and technicians required for various kinds of productions. Although the crew will be running the producer's show, they are contracted by the theatre owner. Theatres that are often used for musicals also have an agreement with the American Federation of Musicians to employ a certain number of musicians, even if none are needed in the production. Musicians needed beyond the stipulated number are contracted by the producer. As you can see, Broadway production is no simple matter.

Thus, people who work in the management areas of commercial theatre not only have to be good with figures, but they also need to be skilled bargainers. Sometimes they have to be very diplomatic; at other times, they should be very firm, but the secret is to know when to be tough and when to be accommodating. Profits and losses will be affected by the deals they make.

The producer's operation is also complicated in the commercial theatre. If he makes his living from producing, rather than being a wealthy person who decides it might be fun to produce a play, he will have his own producing organization. For each show that he produces, he will form a separate producing corporation. This makes for more efficient control, and it is also financially wise. A show that fails disastrously thus can make no claim on the profits of another show that is successful. The staff of one prominent Broadway producer includes the following personnel: General Manager, Production Supervisor, Production Associate, Casting Director, Comptroller, Investor Relations—dealing with the "angels," three personal Assistants for the producer and his deputies, a Production Staff, and some Staff Assistants, not to forget the obligatory typists.

For a specific show, the producer's organization will be headed by a Company Manager, who is responsible for all the administrative details as the producer's representative. He must look to the actors' welfare, as well as see that artistic standards—including discipline—are maintained and generally make sure that there is a good spirit in the ensemble. He needs to be able to get along well with artists but at the same time be firm with them when necessary. He also is responsible for business matters concerning the production and for box office reports. Promotion will be handled by one or more Press Representatives, contracted by the producer. Advertising will be handled by an advertising agency. The show will also need an attorney for legal matters, a firm of accountants, and insurers. The rest of the staff are involved in actual production.

If a successful production tours after its Broadway run, or if it is so successful that a tour company is sent out while the original is still on Broadway, there must be an Advance Manager who precedes the ensemble, making arrangements for publicity, transport, hotel rooms, and special requirements the show may make on each theatre. Even ensembles that are noncommercial, as are a number of dance companies that must tour frequently even to survive, need the services of an Advance Manager.

Small groups may save themselves a lot of effort and expense by allowing an Impresario or a Concert Manager/Management to present them on tour. The late Sol Hurok was one of America's best-known impresarios, specializing in importing major dance and musical groups and soloists from abroad. Columbia Artists Management (CAMI) is now a major power in this field, with management capabilities for ensembles and individual artists in music, dance, and drama. There are, however, a number of other management firms dealing with performing arts bookings and tours. Some are concerned with the college circuit, providing a culturally enriching mixture of the arts for college campuses all over the nation. Some are more interested in community concerts. Some are interested only in bringing major attractions to major theatres or concert halls in major cities. Whatever the scope of the management activities, there is ample opportunity for the staff to work closely with the artists.

Experts who specialize in personal publicity for individual performers have already been mentioned, but this is a challenging field in which some press agents have made themselves both well known and indispensable. Gifted performers are often so busy with their art that they have little time to devote to haggling over contracts, so they may also retain a personal manager to help them plan their engagements and set their fees. If they are making very large fees, as do some opera and theatre/film stars, they may also need an investment expert to help them protect their earnings. Playwrights almost always have literary agents to help them place their plays, obtain good contract terms, collect royalties, and protect their interests in other media.

Another aspect of performing arts management that has recently been developing, thanks in part to the growing interest in subsidized, nonprofit performing ensembles, is that of staffing arts councils and foundation programs devoted to helping the performing arts in America. And, just as theatre architects and technicians hire out their expertise as consultants, so now do management experts. Some can tell you how to reorganize your own staff. Some can tell you how to win foundation grants, federal subsidies, and donations from corporations and the wealthy. Some can tell you the most effective ways to use that money. Some, like Danny Newman, can tell you how to entice more subscribers, how to sell more tickets. Some can advise you on ways to improve your image as an ensemble, or at least your publicity and advertising campaigns.

There is another area of work in the performing arts that isn't performance or technology or management, although one management skill is allied with it. Some arts press representatives began in this area; others give up promotion in favor of it. It is the career of the writer, the critic, the editor, the journalist, who makes him or herself an expert on various of the performing arts and serves them by helping the public to appreciate what they are and what they can mean to our lives. And now, with the ascendancy of television, you can even be an arts critic or reporter without having to write. You can face the camera and tell your unseen audience what is happening in the world of dance or drama. Make no mistake, however, if you criticize and report on the performing arts, you are not supposed to act like a press agent. Honesty, accuracy, knowledge of the arts, high critical standards, and a certain detachment will win you respect in such careers. You don't have to be a Walter Kerr or an Andrew Porter—seasoned, widely admired critics of drama and music—to write reviews. In fact, Porter was quite a young man when he first astonished London readers with his vast knowledge and deep understanding of music and musicians. His fame spread to America, where *The New Yorker* magazine engaged him to review performances both here and abroad. In New York and other cities, young writers have a better chance of being published in community or avant-garde newspapers than in the major papers and magazines. Writing about performance for high school and college newspapers can be good experience.

Some performers will scoff at those who work hard in theatre as managers. Or outside it, as journalists and critics. Some will say that these people just didn't "have what it takes" to become actors, singers, or dancers. What they forget is that not everyone who loves working in the theatre necessarily wants to be in the spotlight. In fact, it's a very wise person who can take a hard look at his abilities and his dreams and make a compromise that will allow him to have a satisfying career in an area he can really master. Unfortunately, there are some so-called professional actors who would have done a much better job if they had been working in the mail room of Lincoln Center. And that is not to imply that processing the mail is a useless, unimportant activity. It can be the lifeline of a theatre, especially in terms of communicating with artists, designers, technicians, supply houses, foundations, and the public—especially the subscribers!

Every job in the theatre has its importance. No theatre job is menial or degrading, insignificant, stupid, boring, unless your attitude toward it makes it so. If attitude is your problem, then even being artistic or technical director will seem boring or menial. The excitement and pride generated by working together with a variety of truly talented people ought to give you a wonderful attitude toward working in the theatre. Your career in the performing arts can be rewarding in many, many ways.

CHAPTER VI

Performing Arts Profiles

BEVERLY SILLS—Artistic Director/Soprano/TV Talk-Show Hostess

When Sir Rudolf Bing was General Manager of the Metropolitan Opera, it was his policy to bring the major stars from Europe. American singers were largely ignored, except for a few who were invited to make debuts at the Met only when their singing careers were virtually over. One deliberate oversight on Sir Rudolf's part excited a lot of criticism. It concerned a lovely young soprano from Brooklyn.

She had had an astonishing success with the critics and the public when the home-grown opera ensemble—the New York City Opera—to which she belonged had moved to Lincoln Center. There in the shiningly golden New York State Theatre, she triumphed as Cleopatra in a revival of a forgotten 18th-century opera by Handel, *Julio Cesare.* Sir Rudolf was not, however, moved to invite this talented and popular soprano to the Met, America's premiere opera stage.

It may have had something to do with the fact that the City Opera had moved from a more distant and very shabby theatre, the City Center, right onto the Met's doorstep in Lincoln Center. Later, however, when this same singer/actress interpreted three British queens—Mary of Scotland, Elizabeth of England, and her mother, Anne Boleyn—on the State Theatre's stage, there was still no invitation from the Met. Sir Rudolf even offered the opinion that being born and raised in Brooklyn doesn't really give you the kind of background you need to perform as a queen on stage.

Beverly Sills showed, however, that she could not only sing and act queens on stage with great power and emotion, but that she could behave offstage with royal grace as well. Not that she was cold and

CHRISTIAN STEINER

Beverly Sills

distant, but rather that she was clearly a star, an impressive talent. But one who was so approachable, so friendly, that she even remembered fans who had come backstage to see her only once or twice. And it was not just her memory that astonished and delighted her public, but the fact that she seemed genuinely pleased to see them. She really wanted to know how they liked the performance. She was touched that they cared enough to take the time to come back after the opera.

She has also performed on comedy TV specials with Carol Burnett. She has been a frequent and charming guest on TV talk shows. What's more, as mistress of ceremonies on a show dealing with current social problems, she has proved herself well informed and wonderfully sympathetic to her panelists and their problems.

How appropriate, then, that the young singer who undertook any role she was asked to do at the old City Center home of the City

Opera is now the Artistic Director of that adventurous and highly admired company. This is a demanding job. She is the first woman to fill it.

Beverly Sills's chance to do this, some might think, was guaranteed because she is so charming, so thoughtful, so beloved. That does have something to do with it, but not all. She is and always has been a very hard worker. She is highly intelligent, a quality that critics at least have accused singers of lacking in some degree. What's more, Beverly began her musical training at the age of seven, in singing. Acting, she says, is an instinct. She doesn't think it can be studied, and her own acting instincts have certainly served her well on stage.

The really hard work has been in mastering roles. Over 130 operas were in Beverly's repertoire before she retired from the stage to take over management of the City Opera in 1979. She learned to speak three languages in addition to English and to sing in even more tongues than that. She is also an accomplished pianist.

So it doesn't really matter whether you are from Brooklyn or Boise. If you have talent and will work hard to perfect it, stardom can be yours.

HAROLD PRINCE—Producer/Director

The Tony is the most coveted award in the American theatre aside from the Pulitzer Prize, which can be won only by playwrights. For everyone else who works in the theatre, the Tony is the top honor. Harold Prince seems to win it with regularity. But he is modest. He has never said, as did a star who had won several: "It's always nice to win one of these."

How has it been possible for a man who began his career in the theatre as a lowly stage manager on *Wonderful Town* to become one of America's most honored, most prolific, and wealthiest producers? How has it been possible, on top of those achievements, to become one of the world's most admired and successful directors of musicals, plays, operas, and films?

Hal Prince's career is truly astonishing. Not just for the chain of successes and the long list of innovations it has given to theatre history, but also for the immense and daring risks he has taken, pushing the content and form of the musical to its outer boundaries. In *Sweeney Todd,* critics seemed to agree, he pushed it all the way over into opera—or perhaps into a new theatre form entirely.

Prince's interest in the theatre, like that of so many successful artists, began in early childhood. It also didn't hurt him to be born into a

Harold Prince

family that knew where the next meal was coming from. In fact, his grandmother had a box at the Metropolitan Opera. As early as the age of six, Hal went to the opera and sat with his grandmother in the box, staring wide-eyed at the wonders on the Met's enormous stage.

At home, he tried making his own operas. He built a miniature stage, designing his own scenery and filling the stage with lead soldiers from the dime store. On Saturdays, when the Texaco broadcasts of operas live from the Met stage were on, Hal would push his soldiers around, recreating the high drama and intense emotion he was hearing on his radio. "I did that every Saturday," he now recalls. "But because I didn't understand the language of most of the operas, sometimes I'd finish the action Milton Cross had described before the singers had finished the score."

Today, Prince's opera stagings are to be seen at the New York City Opera, the Chicago Lyric Opera, and the San Francisco Opera, among other prestigious houses. But he is best known as the producer/director of such shows as *Company, Follies, A Little Night Music, Pacific Overtures, Sweeney Todd,* challenging musicals that have in common the talents of Harold Prince and composer-lyricist Stephen Sondheim. Often other noted names such as Michael Bennett and Hugh Wheeler are also among the credits. Hal Prince likes to work with colleagues whose talents he knows and respects.

Beginning on *Wonderful Town,* sharing the stage manager's tasks with the late Robert Griffith, Hal was bitten by the theatre bug very deeply. He and Griffith decided to try their hand at producing. They worked out plans for *Pajama Game,* another hit musical, while they stage-managed Leonard Bernstein's *Wonderful Town.* Later, Bernstein's *West Side Story* would have Hal Prince as producer, not to mention Stephen Sondheim as lyricist.

If this suggests that it helps your career to meet talented people when you are working in shows, it's true. But you, like Hal Prince, have to be able to take chances and bring the right elements together in the right way at the right time. Even Harold Prince doesn't always seem to do this, at least not to some of the critics' satisfaction. Interestingly, though, critics often admit later that Prince has been ahead of his time. Ahead of his audiences, even ahead of his critics.

CRAIG ANDERSON—Producer

One young producer on his way up is Craig Anderson. His route has not been directly from classroom to Broadway big-time, though in the 1978–79 season two of his productions, originally mounted at his OOBA showcase theatre, the tiny Hudson Guild, were playing on Broadway. They were Hugh Leonard's *Da,* which won seven Tony Awards, and Ernest Thompson's *On Golden Pond.* Anderson grew up in southern California, not far from film and television studios, where he appeared in some teen-age roles. He says he knew he didn't have what it takes to be a really good actor, though he wasn't a bad one.

In his adult career, however, he wanted to do whatever he did with excellence. He decided he wanted to be a producer when he realized how many good scripts never get a good production—or even a bad one. In order to learn as much as he could about how the theatre works, he studied—and taught—theatre at UCLA. He was then able to work with director Gordon Davidson at the Mark Taper Forum in Los Angeles. Going East, he worked at the Vivian Beaumont Theatre

Craig Anderson

in Lincoln Center and at New Haven's Long Wharf Theatre, mastering many aspects of theatre production and financing.

When he felt he was ready to try his hand at packaging play productions, he took over the direction of the drama program at the Hudson Guild, a community center playhouse with only 120 seats. Yet, working with skill and charm, he got designers such as Ming Cho Lee, directors like Melvin Bernhardt, and performers of the caliber of Barnard Hughes, Shirley Knight, and Tammy Grimes to give him their best—for almost no monetary return. His promise: that if any show moved to Broadway, it would move *intact,* and everybody who had made it possible would have their well-deserved financial reward. In many transfers, some lose out, replaced by producers looking for a "bigger name."

In one season while still at the Hudson Guild, Anderson had to turn away over 30,000 people who wanted to see his short-run showcases. When *On Golden Pond* opened on Broadway in the renovated Apollo, long a "grind" movie house, Anderson's production was pre-

John Neumeier

sented by a senior production team of Arthur Cantor and Greer Garson, who raised the money. But he was on his way—and in good company.

JOHN NEUMEIER—Artistic Director/Choreographer

There's an old saying that a prophet is often without honor in his own country. The people who knew you as a child won't listen to you when you are a man. You have to go elsewhere to have your words and your work taken seriously.

That has certainly proved to be the case with John Neumeier, who at one time was the youngest ballet director in Europe. This was in Frankfurt, West Germany, *not* in America, his homeland. Born in Milwaukee, Wisconsin, Neumeier early had an interest in dancing and was supported by his family. But, aside from dancing in musicals, there was not much work, since openings in major ballet ensembles were limited. Even on Broadway, the employment was not—and still is not—regular.

In England, Neumeier performed in the London production of *West Side Story,* in the astonishing, innovative dances of Jerome Robbins, who also choreographs for the New York City Ballet. This brought his talent to the attention of the late John Cranko, artistic director and major choreographer for the much admired Stuttgart Ballet. Cranko contracted Neumeier for the Stuttgart ensemble, not only developing him as a leading dancer, but encouraging him as a creator of dances as well.

Neumeier's work was so highly praised, so early, that the Frankfurt Opera wanted no one else to take charge of their company. The job was a very demanding one in several ways. The basic work of the Frankfurt Opera Ballet was to provide the dance sequences that are all too brief a part of many operas. But that can be very discouraging to highly trained dancers who would love to do a full-length *Swan Lake,* not merely six minutes in *Aida.*

The Stuttgart Ballet had once been a company like that, intended to dress up the opera stage for a few minutes every other night. Neumeier created exciting new ballets for his dancers and insisted that they have full evenings, often alternating with the operas. In Frankfurt, he began giving old, famed classical ballets *new* stories and new choreography. His version of Stravinsky's *Firebird* was like "Buck Rogers in the 25th century."

German critics and audiences were shocked at first, but soon both the experts and the people who buy the tickets were cheering. Neumeier became famous so fast that he was invited to Hamburg to make the opera ballet there into a major company. He has done this. The company not only has its share of evenings on the stage of the Hamburg State Opera, but it tours internationally as well.

He has been begged to come to Munich to head its ballet. Other ballets and opera ensembles have asked him to work with them. When he has the time in a very busy schedule, he will choreograph a new work—or one of his older ones already in the Hamburg repertoire—for other ballet troupes. So now, with Neumeier dances in the programs of some important American and Canadian companies, he is at last winning the honors he deserves in his own land.

One summer, he was invited to do the most important choreography for three of Europe's most important festivals: Munich, Bayreuth, and Salzburg. But such honors abroad are tinged with sadness for Neumeier, who learned his German in Germany, not in Milwaukee. "Every time I go back to America," he says, "it seems to me almost a tragedy. I

CHRISTIAN STEINER

Rita Shane

see such incredibly good talent, but it's almost hopeless. There isn't enough *outlet.* There isn't enough *need.* An art can only exist where there's a need for it. It can't just be frosting on the cultural cake."

RITA SHANE—Soprano

Even in times of equal opportunity, it is still difficult for a young woman to have a performance career if she also wants to have a family. This is especially true for singers, who must often travel to fulfill concert engagements and tour with opera ensembles. They also usually work at night, just when their husbands and children would like to have them at home. The key to success is an understanding husband and children who adore and admire their mother for being both artist and mom.

Rita Shane, who sings major roles at the Met and the City Opera, as well as at important opera houses abroad, says she never would have had a career at all had it not been for her husband. They met in college, when they joined a Gilbert and Sullivan production group. Then they were both amateurs, with no thought of being paid for singing. After college, Rita worked for the Metropolitan Opera Auditions as a secretary.

If her life had been like a Hollywood film, she would have stepped out from behind her desk and dazzled the judges with her remarkable voice. No such thing! She never even told her employers that she liked to sing. Her husband, Dan Tritter, insisted she try for a career. He knew she had real talent. He says he didn't want to have her look back with regret, thinking that she could have had a career if only she hadn't married and had a family.

It was loving and generous of Dan Tritter to support his wife in her continued singing lessons and auditions. But he did more. He even went with her to Santa Fe, New Mexico, where she was to spend a summer as an apprentice, learning more about opera performance. What happened in Santa Fe *was* like a movie. One day while she was sunning by the pool, a call came for her to report to the open-air theatre. The star for that evening's performance of Strauss's *Die Fledermaus* had been taken ill. Could she sing Rosalinda on very short notice?

She could—and she did, to bravos. Her career was on the way. It has included such demanding roles as the Queen of the Night in Mozart's *The Magic Flute* and such lovely lyric ones as Violetta in Verdi's *La Traviata.* Rita has even sung the role of Olympia, the mechanical doll in Offenbach's *Tales of Hoffmann,* on roller skates!

Rita Shane is an outstanding example of the new breed of American opera singers, young talents who can sing, dance, and act and who are not afraid to try something new and different if it will make the opera more effective theatrically. But she is also a wife and mother who chooses her engagements carefully so she can have plenty of time with her family. Whenever Dan Tritter and son Michael can, however, they take a brief holiday and go along with their favorite opera star.

JOHN LEE BEATTY—Set and Costume Designer

"One of my greatest ambitions," says young designer John Lee Beatty, "is to get some sleep." It's not that he suffers from insomnia, but that

John Lee Beatty

he has too much work to do in the theatre. "I'm on the run all the time," he says. At a time when noted Broadway designers are lucky to have one show a season, Beatty's work is being seen all around the town. By the end of the 1970's, he was working on as many as sixteen separate shows. Even before that, as what he himself calls "a child wonder," he was averaging twelve shows.

And why does this pleasant and somewhat shy designer get so much work? Does he give producers special rates? Not at all. The union wouldn't allow that, and Beatty believes that he and all his colleagues should be fairly paid for their artistry. The secret is that Beatty is very good, very versatile, and also a very fast worker. This is especially astonishing, since it takes time to conceive and develop an original idea for setting a play and even more time to make color sketches, build detailed models, and draft exact plans. Not to mention working out costume plates and the colors and fabrics that should be used in building the costumes.

What's more, John Lee Beatty does much of the work himself. He thinks it is a fault that he must correct, he says, but he does find it hard to delegate some of his work to assistants. Yet he knows that that is one of the best ways for young designers to get started. He himself worked with Ming Cho Lee, the famed Broadway designer. He studied design with Lee at the Yale School of Drama after undergraduate studies at Brown University. He has also worked with another noted Lee alumnus, designer Douglas Schmidt.

Not only does a young talent learn a lot about how an artist works—and about the often difficult practical circumstances of working on a professional show—with designers such as Lee or Schmidt, but there's another dividend, too. Such noted artists are always in demand. When they have too much work, they are apt to be generous and let an assistant whose skills they admire do a design commission.

John Lee Beatty's desire to be a stage designer was born at the early age of seven when he was taken to see *Peter Pan.* Unlike many children who want to fly—or at least act—after seeing that beloved show, Beatty's only dream was to design.

Now he is a regular designer for the Goodspeed Opera House (CN) revivals of old musical comedies. He is also almost a "family" designer for ensembles such as Circle Repertory, the Public Theatre, and the Manhattan Theatre Club.

"When I started getting successful," he recalls, "it was a big surprise. Not like a shock, but all of a sudden you wake up one day and people want you. The telephone doesn't stop ringing. You get chances to do shows you've always wanted to do. Or directors you like working with ask you to do another show with them. That's what surprises me about the career. It leads you around by the nose—not the other way around."

GIL WECHSLER—Lighting Designer

Shocking though it may seem, there are some opera stage directors who cannot read a musical score. That being so, how much less musical training can be expected of designers and technicians working on ballet and opera productions. Then along comes Gil Wechsler, recently lighting designer for Canada's Stratford Festival and now for the Metropolitan Opera. Wechsler not only can read a score, but he can also play an instrument—the accordion, which he studied because his family couldn't afford a piano when he was in elementary school. Later, in high school, he was able to study the piano. He didn't know then how useful it would be to him as a lighting designer to be able to read a ballet or opera score, not only for simple things like matching light cues to specific notes or timing fades through musical transitions, but for the more complex problems of creating mood and milieu, of subtly reinforcing the dramatic tensions.

Wechsler recalls seeing hundreds of shows of all kinds, even as a

JACK MITCHELL

Gil Wechsler

high school student. Living in New York City, that wasn't difficult to manage. But, he says, he always thought of the theatre as a diversion, a hobby rather than a possible vocation. So he majored in physics at Rensselaer Polytechnic Institute for nearly four years. "But I realized it had nothing to do with people," Gil admits. "It was all right for 8 hours a day, but not for 24. I wanted something that would interest me all the time. Like theatre."

He chose New York University for training. It was located in the theatre center, of course, but it also allowed him to concentrate on lighting as well as acting and directing, in which he was equally interested at the time. At NYU, he reinforced the musical emphasis in his training. A fellow student, working with the New York City Ballet, invited him to a performance. "He said I could wear jeans and sneak down from the balcony to the second mezzanine where all the dancers were sitting," Wechsler remembers. "The opening ballet was *The Prodigal Son,* and there were tears streaming down my face. The others looked at me as though I were crazy. They'd all seen it a hundred times. To them it was nothing—just movement.

"To me, that ballet was the synthesis of a great number of things. The last ballet on the program was *Symphony in C,* which is just pure movement to music. Again, I was completely overwhelmed. I started going every night, as Edward Gorey, the cartoonist and designer of *Dracula,* does. At that point, ballet meant a great deal to me. Music, movement, and light began to come together for me; they became something that was and is a part of my life. I also studied dancing and singing, as well as acting, not because I wanted to become a professional, but because I wanted to know about what they involved."

Wechsler found that he could start working Off Broadway after NYU, but he felt he still didn't know enough about theatre to work as a professional. So he went to the Yale School of Drama. Oddly enough, he enrolled as a directing major, but he wasn't happy with either that program or the one in acting. He had been doing lighting on an amateur basis for years and was annoyed that he was not allowed to take an advanced lighting class because he was in directing. "So I helped lead a student revolution at Yale to change things, to put them on a more professional basis. To get into that lighting class I finally had to say, OK, I'm not a director, I'm a lighting designer."

While at Yale, Gil was beginning to do Off Broadway ballet lighting, getting practical experience. The British designer Michael Annals, then teaching at Yale, asked Wechsler to go to London with him briefly to supervise sets and costumes and create the lighting for a new Anthony Tudor ballet, *Shadow Play,* which was being premiered at Covent Garden by the Royal Ballet. If Wechsler is working for top organizations now, he has a precedent: he started at the top.

After Yale, there were some months as Jo Mielziner's assistant, doing drafting and lighting. Gil did the light plots for the ill-fated *Mata Hari.* Following this, he had his own Broadway show to light: Charles Dyer's *Staircase,* with Eli Wallach and Milo O'Shea.

His first exposure to the also ill-fated Harkness Ballet came about the same time. "I thought everything was wonderful—except the lighting. I met the director, Brian MacDonald, and told him so. He said, 'Okay, you should be our lighting designer.' " For two years, which included two U.S. tours and a European circuit, Wechsler lit the Harkness. When the company was deactivated, he relit the rep of the Pennsylvania Ballet. Then Michael Annals called him to Canada, where the Stratford Festival was producing *Satyricon,* which the former lighting designer said couldn't be lit. He did it, and Stratford asked him to light their fall tour that year, 1969. Since then, he's been a Stratford regular and currently is also head of lighting at the Metropolitan Opera.

Lindsay Gambini

LINDSAY GAMBINI—Performing Arts Manager

When young people first become involved in the performing arts, they get the impression that all the excitement is on the stage. Lindsay Gambini is a young woman with the talent and vitality to become a musical comedy star, but once she tasted the experience of managing and producing performances, she realized she wanted to do more.

At the age of fourteen, Lindsay started out with the Encore Theatre in Chicago. "I was cast in *The Sound of Music* and grew up playing the different children in the show. Then I did summer stock when I was fifteen, sixteen, seventeen, eighteen, and twenty." Even though theatre was Lindsay's first love, she followed the advice of her family and obtained a BA in sociology and teaching credentials.

Instead of teaching, she plunged back into the theatre. Eventually, while working with an experimental theatre in California, she set out with two friends to bring a summer stock company to Bethany, Pennsylvania. Lindsay admits, "I had a friend who kept encouraging me to go into arts administration, but at that time I didn't know what it was!"

At the Bethany Colony Playhouse, Lindsay acquired a taste for the excitement behind the lights as well as out front. She ended up supervising the administrative, artistic, and box office staff, managing press relations as well as handling the payroll and budgets. "We learned a lot by the seat of our pants," she says. "I discovered I was as excited about making it happen as I was by being in the shows."

Lindsay wanted more background in management. She earned a Master of Fine Arts in Performing Arts Administration at New York University, studying Theatre as well as Marketing, Accounting, and Advertising Management. After graduation she landed a job at the Stage Company in Flushing, New York, as Managing Director. Since that time, Lindsay has worked for John Houseman's The Acting Company in Manhattan, where she started as Promotion Director and became Assistant General Manager. She was Managing Director of the Circle Repertory, an Off Broadway company, before moving to her present position as Associate Director, Performing Arts Division, Opportunity Resources for the Arts. Lindsay is responsible for the Theatre/Performing Arts program of this nationwide nonprofit placement center for arts administrators.

Lindsay Gambini's career illustrates the great demand for talented arts administrators. "Don't be afraid to be specific in your career. Tell organizations what you can do for them," she advises.

Currently, Lindsay is also a candidate for a PhD at the City University of New York. Her long-term goal is to manage her own producing organization.

JOSEPH VOLPE—Director of Operations, Metropolitan Opera Association

"Working in the theatre was just a freak accident," says Joseph Volpe, Director of Operations for the Metropolitan Opera. Volpe graduated from Stony Brook Prep on Long Island in 1958 and went into automobile body repair. Skipping college, he worked for Maserati of

LAWRENCE S. EPSTEIN

Joseph Volpe

America until he decided to go into business with a friend. But, while waiting several weeks before going into business, he got a job backstage at the Morosco Theatre. He liked it so much that he forgot about the business idea, took an exam given by IATSE Local One, and became a carpenter's apprentice at the Metropolitan Opera.

"I didn't even know what an opera was," says Volpe. "I became interested in taking an apprenticeship and learning the trade." He worked his way up from apprentice carpenter to journeyman, moving with the Met in 1966 from its original location to its present home at Lincoln Center. For many years, he worked during the day as a carpenter at the Met and at night as a stagehand on Broadway. Finally, he became a master carpenter and, eventually, the Met's Technical Director. He now holds the position of Director of Operations, an extremely complicated and demanding job.

Joseph Volpe is responsible for over three hundred employees, and he works directly with the major department heads of the Met, including the three stage departments, the scene shop, and the construction shops. "When I first started, I just wanted to do the best job I could," he says.

"You should get as much background and knowledge as you can in high school and college," he advises. "You have to be excited about the challenge of solving a problem. If you can be successful in the theatre, you can be successful anywhere."

Volpe enjoys working at the Met. He is proud that the Met, in spite of time and economic limitations, has the "tremendous resources" of its creative staff to produce fabulous sets on schedule. After helping to build or produce over 125 operas, he can tell you of the long hours that anyone committed to a theatrical career must devote to his work. "Just to learn the Met operation, familiarize yourself with the people who work here, and study union regulations would take two years."

LYNN MONTGOMERY—Production Director

Lynn Montgomery is Production Director of New York's Equity Library Theatre. ELT, as it is popularly known, produces revivals of well-known plays and gives AEA (Actors' Equity Association) members an opportunity to be seen by casting agents and critics, as well as by general audiences. Lynn Montgomery supervises eight major productions a year, each with a different cast, director, and crew. All are volunteers!

Lynn began her involvement in theatre as a teenager in Springfield, Massachusetts. In community theatres, she acted, directed, produced, stage-managed, painted scenery, and handled properties. She cites 1959 as the start of her professional career, the year she graduated from Columbia University's School of Dramatic Arts with a B.F.A. in Theatre Production.

Before joining ELT, Lynn worked in a variety of stage-management and arts-management positions with several theatres: The Green Mountain Theatre, Vermont; the Lakewood Theatre, Maine; the Cleveland Musicarnival, Ohio; and the Palm Beach Musicarnival, Florida. She was stage manager for many summer stock companies, such as the Cape Playhouse, the North Shore Music Theatre, and the Berkshire Theatre Festival. She also was a stage manager for the Professional Theatre Program at the University of Michigan.

When Lynn came to New York to work as a professional, she didn't find it easy. She says, "I held body and soul together working for

McGraw-Hill, at office temporaries, and at the Ballet Theatre School as a secretary. I was, at one point, the Executive Secretary of the Oratorio Society of New York." She also worked as a secretary for several New York producers, all the while working in summer stock seasons outside New York. Before she joined ELT, Lynn Montgomery had worked on the stage-management staff of *Slow Dance on the Killing Ground* Off Broadway and on two Broadway shows, *Brief Lives* and *Georgy.*

Lynn Montgomery

Now, in addition to her work at ELT, Lynn Montgomery teaches stage management at Brooklyn College.

Lynn says that a stage manager is "a person who is essentially responsible for the mechanics of the production and seeing that all departments function as they should. I feel that women are particularly suited to be stage managers and very often they make very good stage managers; the barriers are down."

At ELT, Lynn works with interns from high schools and colleges as well as with professional theater artists. She talks with hundreds of young actors, directors, stage managers, and designers who come to audition for the chance to have their work seen at ELT.

If you make the theatre your career, you may meet Lynn Montgomery sooner than you think.

SUSAN BLOCH—Public Relations Expert

Although slight of stature and mild-mannered, Susan Bloch is one of New York's most active press and public relations experts. Unlike some high-pressure PR agents who live by the "hype," Ms. Bloch represents only those productions, ensembles, or personalities whose artistry she admires. Thus, she can write glowing advertising copy for them without having to feel she is fibbing. She was born and raised in a small town in upstate New York. Her first interest in the arts surfaced with discovery of talent in painting. Later, she studied sculpture in Sri Lanka—formerly Ceylon. She has also been a pilot of single-engine airplanes, an appropriate hobby for a high-flying profession such as public relations.

Susan's work in press agentry has been so effective that the Outer Critics Circle has voted her an award. She's also on the boards of New York's Chelsea Theatre and Playhouse Repertory and has been a consultant to FEDAPT and the N.Y. State Council on the Arts.

Currently, she runs Susan Bloch and Company, specializing in service to cultural organizations such as theatre and dance groups. She describes the work as "active, always pressured, and often satisfying, as one has the quiet delight of seeing hundreds of hours of labor, calculation, writing, meetings, and planning translate into long- and short-term public achievement for the client."

Ms. Bloch stresses that neither she nor most of her generation of public relations and arts promotion experts consciously chose their careers. Today, things are different. Such skills are now taught—now and then by Ms. Bloch, both to her apprentices and to college classes.

The primary abilities needed for her job, she emphasizes, are seldom discussed in classrooms. They include writing *and* typing skills, the ability to see a story in the making and to interpret it well, the strength and discipline for very long workdays, and a life very closely identified with one's career. It also helps to serve the required apprenticeship under capable union members to earn the ATPAM union card. This allows its holder to be a General Press Representative for legitimate theatrical productions under union contracts on and Off Broadway.

Even without formal training in press representation, Susan has found that her college curriculum was good preparation. Studies in English, especially drama, introduced her to the performing arts, to effective

Susan Bloch

writing, to the necessary skills of analysis and organization that a busy press agent must possess. Her work in science enhanced her sense of analysis and planning, as well as developing her skills as a researcher. Added to these course-work dividends was experience gained in extra-curricular activities as she followed her love of the stage, discovered an emerging talent for graphics and painting, and found she had a real gift for bringing order out of chaos.

Something else important: Susan Bloch did not want to be a Star. She knew she wanted to work in the performing arts, but behind the scenes, to contribute to creative expression without adulation or applause. Not everyone enjoys such a position.

Here's how she got her first job: "A year out of college, I was urged to interview for a position as Gal Friday and assistant to the Public Relations Director for the newly conceived Lincoln Center Repertory group, to be headed by Robert Whitehead and Elia Kazan. After landing the job—which is always a combination of luck and timing, as well as disposition—the guiding principle was 'sink or swim.' "

Her good fortune was to work under one of Broadway's most experienced press agents, Barry Hyams, who had represented Sol Hurok's many attractions. Hyams gave her as much responsibility as she could carry. He didn't teach her what to do, though. He did his job, and she learned by his example. In three years, Susan Bloch was made Director of Public Relations for the Repertory Theatre of Lincoln Center, a position she held for a decade, discharging her many duties with efficiency and unfailing friendliness no matter what the pressures. Since the company was then the nation's largest repertory theatre, with two stages, touring engagements, and an impressive program of plays each season, there was much to do; all publicity, promotion, graphics, editorial programs, and interviews were supervised by Ms. Bloch.

Today, she says of this and similar challenges: "During those years, I developed craft and garnered invaluable on-the-job experience. Working conscientiously in publicity, public information, and promotion in the arts can prepare you for any number of careers in arts administration. The particular challenge and exhilaration in this field is the rich knowledge it requires in all areas—and the fact that one's job is as far-reaching as one's own boundaries."

When the late Jules Irving resigned as Artistic Director of the Repertory Theatre, to be replaced by Joseph Papp, Susan went to Janus Films as Director of Creative Programming, proving her point about the varied careers open to people in public relations. At Janus, she set up the first feature-film library for America's public television stations. She was also a consultant to the National Endowment for the Humanities on institutional public relations.

So many people and groups asked her for advice and aid in publicizing their work that she finally set up her own shop to provide this service. There are compensations in running your own business in public relations, but you are, she stresses, responsible for finding and maintaining accounts—and for making sure that all who work with and for you are looked after. When you work for an agency, you don't have so many responsibilities. But those are choices that depend on each person's nature and needs.

APPENDIX A

Theatrical Organizations

These organizations are part of the professional support provided for the performing arts community. Some of their publications are available free and others at low cost. These are the places to go for career help and information. You may wish to write them for their latest publications and to be placed on their mailing lists.

American Theatre Association
1000 Vermont Avenue, N.W.
Washington, DC 20005
Provides college information and yearly summer theatre directories. The ATA runs a placement service for members and can be important throughout your career.

Association of Hispanic Arts
200 East 87th Street
New York, NY 10028
Publishes a bimonthly newsletter.

Black Theatre Alliance
410 West 42nd Street
New York, NY 10036
Publishes a monthly newsletter and other publications.

Chicago Alliance for the Performing Arts
176 West Adams Street, Suite 2010
Chicago, IL 60603
Publishes a monthly newsletter and other publications.

Foundation for the Extension and Development of the American Professional Theatre
165 West 46th Street
New York, NY 10016
Nonprofit organization that gives counseling and managerial advice to professional theatre projects. They have several good publications that you may purchase to help guide you in managing your own theatre program.

Institute of Outdoor Drama
University of North Carolina
202 Graham Memorial 052-A
Chapel Hill, NC 27514
Provides a complete list of the outdoor dramas in the U.S. These productions, usually staged during the summer, often hire beginners and theatre apprentices.

League of Professional Theatre Training Programs
1860 Broadway
New York, NY 10023
Offers training programs in various aspects of theatre. Provides a pamphlet listing programs in colleges and universities.

League of Resident Theatres
c/o The Guthrie Theatre
725 Vineland Place
Minneapolis, MN 55403
Publishes a list of Equity theatres.

Los Angeles Theatre Alliance
6253 Hollywood Blvd., Suite 315
Los Angeles, CA 90038
A good place to find out what is happening in the area's nonprofit theatre.

Off Off Broadway Alliance
325 Spring Street, Room 315
New York, NY 10013
Offers a list of about 50 Off Off Broadway theatres.

Opportunity Resources for the Arts
1501 Broadway, Suite 2605
New York, NY 10036

Nonprofit organization that provides placement service for arts administrators. There is a small fee.

P.E.N. American Center
156 Fifth Avenue
New York, NY 10010
Publishes *Grants and Awards,* listing those available to all playwrights.

Theatre Communications Group
355 Lexington Avenue
New York, NY 10017
Publishes directories, books, and newsletters at low cost.

University/Resident Theatre Association
1540 Broadway
New York, NY 10036
Organizers of the National Unified Auditions. These auditions, held in locations around the country, provide access to training opportunities in acting, directing, technical production, management, promotion, publicity, and directing. Write for the list of participating universities and theatres and for information on audition qualifications.

APPENDIX B

Unions

Unions can be categorized as performing unions and craft unions. The entire union situation can be very confusing, even to experienced contract negotiators. Many performers are members of more than one union, such as Actors' Equity Association and the American Federation of Television and Radio Artists. If the performer is a carpenter as well, an International Alliance of Stage Employees card is also required. There are even special unions such as the Hebrew Actors Union and the Italian Actors Union.

As you progress in your career you will learn which union you should join. Often it is unwise to join a union just to "have a card." Many young actors and actresses obtain Equity cards after landing a role in an Equity-approved production. However, it then becomes impossible for them to audition for roles in nonunion productions, which would include the majority of roles available to them.

Write or call the unions for information about local chapters in your area, membership requirements, and fees and dues.

Actors' Equity Association (AEA)
165 West 46th Street
New York, NY 10036

AEA, or "Equity," as it is often called, is the union for stage actors. AEA contracts with Broadway, Off Broadway, summer stock, children's theatre, the League of Resident Theatres, dinner theatres, industrial shows, and showcases.

The initiation fee is high, and dues vary according to income. There is an apprenticeship program; ask your drama teacher or write to AEA. Remember that you may wish to work for a time in nonunion shows such as Off Off Broadway theatres before joining Equity. Usually, one may join Equity by auditioning for and being cast in an AEA-approved production. Equity shows also have AEA stage managers.

The AEA is a nationwide union and is one of the performing unions in the Associated Actors and Artists of America (AFL–CIO), which relates the performing unions to each other. The member unions are AEA, American Guild of Musical Artists (AGMA), American Guild of Variety Artists (AGVA), Screen Actors Guild (SAG), Screen Extras Guild (SEG), Hebrew Actors Union, and Italian Actors Union.

American Federation of Television and Radio Artists (AFTRA)
1350 Avenue of the Americas
New York, NY 10019

AFTRA is an open-membership union that accepts all who apply for membership. Initiation fees are based on the area where the applicant resides. The dues are based on income levels in the fields of radio, TV, nonbroadcast materials, transcriptions, videotaped commercial recordings, cassettes, and phonograph records. AFTRA represents actors and actresses, singers, dancers, announcers, newscasters, narrators, lecturers, commentators, analysts, masters of ceremonies, sound-effects artists, demonstrators, moderators, quizmasters, disc jockeys, sportscasters, specialty acts, puppeteers, walkons, and extras. At certain TV and radio stations, AFTRA also represents news and continuity writers.

American Guild of Musical Artists (AGMA)
1841 Broadway
New York, NY 10036

AGMA represents a relatively small (approximately 5,000) membership of "musical artists in the classical field." AGMA is the union of ballet dancers, modern dancers, and opera and choral singers. Its members may also have to belong to another union. For example, a dancer from the New York City Ballet who appeared in a Broadway musical would have to belong to Equity as well as AGMA. The AGMA dues are based upon earnings. You can join AGMA if you are offered a job in a company that has signed the AGMA contract.

American Guild of Variety Artists (AGVA)
1540 Broadway
New York, NY 10036

The AGVA contracts cover nightclubs, resort hotels, cruise ships, and circuses. The performers represented include all kinds of variety talent such as rock, pop, folk singers, comedians, dancers, magicians, acrobatic teams, and animal acts. AGVA is an open union.

American Federation of Musicians (AFM)
1500 Broadway
New York, NY 10036

The AFM is the union for musicians in any part of the entertainment industry. It is the largest performing union, with over 300,000 members. The union negotiates contracts with nightclubs, the Broadway stage, orchestras, network radio and TV, phonograph records, TV films, non-theatrical non-TV documentary films, and industrial films. The AFM has locals nationwide, and initiation fees range from a low of $11 to over $200. The dues vary according to the region. The program "Young Sounds of the AFM" is open to young musicians between 14 and 21. This provides all the benefits of membership at a reduced initiation fee and rate of dues. After 90 days "Young Sounds" members may change their minds and get full refunds. Music group members under 14 can become associate members free.

Association of Theatrical Press Agents and Managers (ATPAM)
268 West 47th Street
New York, NY 10036

Company managers, house managers, and press agents on Broadway and Off Broadway must belong to ATPAM. There are only two ways to join ATPAM: you can apprentice, or you may be in a job over which ATPAM wants to gain jurisdiction. This is one of the most difficult unions to enter and often requires personal contacts. Outside of New York City, ATPAM membership is not required for most management positions. Sometimes, work in summer stock can persuade an ATPAM manager or press agent to invite you to be an ATPAM apprentice.

Directors Guild of America
234 West 44th Street
New York, NY 10036

Future directors or even production assistants may wish to contact the Directors Guild. The initiation fees run from $200 for a production assistant to $2,000 for a director, plus a percentage of the director's salary.

Dramatists Guild
234 West 44th Street
New York, NY 10036

If you have written a full-length play, you may want to join the Dramatists Guild. The Guild also wishes to hear from you if you have had your play produced. The membership fee is low. The Guild is the originator of the Minimum Basic Production Contract, an important document should your play ever come to the Broadway stage.

International Alliance of Theatrical Stage Employees (IATSE)
1515 Broadway
New York, NY 10036

The full name of IATSE is The International Alliance of Theatrical Stage Employees and Moving Picture Machine Operators of the United States and Canada. IATSE represents stage employees, treasurers, ticket sellers, theatrical wardrobe attendants, makeup artists, and hair stylists. Under the category of stage employees are stagehands, carpenters, property people, electricians, and all the personnel in their various departments. IATSE has over fifty separate contracts. Write to IATSE concerning its apprenticeship program.

Screen Actors Guild (SAG)
551 Fifth Avenue
New York, NY 10017

If you want to work in films as well as on stage, you will eventually have to join SAG. It is not an easy union to join, since it has difficulty keeping the majority of its current membership employed.

Society of Stage Directors and Choreographers (SSDC)
1350 Broadway
New York, NY 10036

SSDC helps directors and choreographers by negotiating a minimum basic contract, although most contracts are negotiated on a case-by-case basis.

United Scenic Artists of America (USA)
1540 Broadway
New York, NY 10036

USA represents designers and their assistants as well as scenic artists. USA holds examinations for membership from January to March for scenic artists, costume designers, and lighting designers. Joining USA is a long process; after passing the exam you will be interviewed, you will have to submit a design project, and then you will be voted on by USA judges. Only internationally known designers or a designer who must be hired on the insistence of a producer can be admitted without the examination. The initiation fee runs from $500 to $2,500 depending upon your field and your method of obtaining membership.

APPENDIX C

Summer Stock Theatres

The summer stock theatres listed below operate under Actors' Equity contracts. Often they employ young people as apprentices. Other summer theatres include many nonunion performance groups. A complete, state-by-state listing of summer theatres may be obtained by writing for the annual Summer Theatre Director of the American Theatre Association, 1000 Vermont Avenue NW, Washington, DC.

Adams Memorial Theatre
Box 517
Williamstown, MA 01267

Aldelphi University
Olmstead Theatre
Garden City, NY 11530

Adirondack Playhouse Inc.
Playhouse on the Hill
Clinton, NY 13323

Academy Festival
Lake Forest, IL 60045

Allenberry Playhouse
Boiling Springs, PA 17007

American Stage Festival
Box 225
Milford, NH 03055

Atlanta Civic Center
P.O. Box 11748
Atlanta, GA 30305

Barn Theatre
Augusta, MI 49012

Barry Tuttle Summer Theatre
East Rochester, NY 14603

The Barnstormers
Tamworth, NH 03886

Berkshire Playhouse
East Main Street
Stockbridge, MA 01262

Bill-Bart Enterprises Inc.
Theatre East on Oakland
Milwaukee, WI 53211

Brunswick Music Theatre
Bowdoin Campus
Brunswick, ME 04011

Candlewood Area Theatre
New Fairfield, CT 06810

Cape Cod Melody Tent
Hyannis, MA 02601

Cape Playhouse
Dennis, MA

Casa Manana
3101 West Lancaster
Fort Worth, TX 76107

Casino Theatre
Union Plaza Hotel
1 Main Street
Las Vegas, NV 89101

Cecilwood Theatre
Route 52, Main Street
P.O. Box 56
Fishkill, NY 12524

The Charles Playhouse
76 Warrenton Street
Boston, MA 02116

Chateau Louise Resort Theatre
West Dundee, IL 60118

Civil Light Opera
Heniz Hall
600 Pennsylvania Avenue
Pittsburgh, PA 15222

Corning Summer Theatre
P.O. Box 51
Corning, NY 14830

Dallas Summer Musicals
P.O. Box 26188
Dallas, TX 75226

Drury Lane Theatre at the Water
175 East Chestnut Street
Chicago, IL 60611

Drury Lane East McCormick
Place
Chicago, IL 60611

Drury Lane Theatre South
2500 West 94th Place
Evergreen Park, IL 60642

Elitch Gardens Theatre
4620 West 38th Avenue
Denver, CO 80212

Falmouth Playhouse
Falmouth, MA 02541

Flat Rock Playhouse
Flat Rock, NC 28731

Goodspeed Opera House
East Haddam, CT 06423

Hampton Playhouse
Hampton, NH 03103

Highlands Playhouse
P.O. Box 896
Highlands, NC 28741

Ivoryton Playhouse
Ivoryton, CT 06442

John Drew Theatre
158 Main Street
East Hampton, NY 11937

Kenley Players
Memorial Hall
East First Street
Dayton, OH 45402

Kresge Theatre
Carnegie-Mellon University
College of Fine Arts
Pittsburgh, PA 15213

Lakes Region Playhouse
P.O. Box 199
Weirs Beach
Gilford, NY 13246

Lakewood Theatre
P.O. Box 99
Skowhegan, ME 04976

Lexington Conservatory Theatre
Box 127
Lexington, NY 12452

Lindenwood College
Lindenwood State Company
St. Charles, MO 63301

Little Theatre on the Square
Box 155
Sullivan, IL 61951

Marriott's Lincolnshire Resort
Theatre
Lincolnshire, IL 60015

Milwaukee Melody Tent
710 Plankinton Avenue
Milwaukee, WI 53223

Mountain Playhouse
Jennerstown, PA 15547

Mule Barn Theatre
Tarkio College
Tarkio, MO 64491

North Shore Music Theatre
P.O. Box 62
Beverly, MA 01915

Newport Actor's Company
Breadway Inn
America's Cup Avenue
Newport, RI 02840

Ogunquit Playhouse
Ogunquit, ME 03907

O. J. Thomas Hall
Akron University
Akron, OH 44325

Old Log Theatre
Box 250
Excelsior, MN 55331

Olney Theatre
Route 108
Olney, MD 20832

Palm Springs Center Theatre
P.O. Box 1953
Palm Springs, CA 92262

Paper Mill Playhouse
Brookside Drive
Millburn, NJ 07041

Parker Playhouse
Holiday Park
Fort Lauderdale, FL 33304

Peninsula Players
Highway 42
Fishcreek, WI 54212

Peterborough Playhouse
Off Middle Hancock Road
Peterborough, NH 03458

Picky Video Corp.
Cherry County Playhouse

Box 661
Traverse City, MI 49684

Playhouse-in-the-Park
West Fairmont Park
Philadelphia, PA 19131

Playhouse-on-the-Mall
Bergen Mall Shopping Center
Paramus, NJ 07642

Pocono Playhouse
Mountainome, PA 19432

Red Barn Theatre
Saugatuck, MI 49453

Royal Poinciana Plaza
P.O. Box 231
Palm Beach, FL 33480

Sacramento Music Circus
1419 H Street
Sacramento, CA 95184

St. Louis Municipal Opera
Forest Park
St. Louis, MO 63112

St. Michael's Playhouse
56 College Parkway
Winooski, VT 05404

Shady Lane Playhouse
Route 20 West
Marengo, IL 60152

Sharon Playhouse
Route 396
Sharon, CT 06069

Smithville Theatre
Route 9
Smithville, NJ 08201

Starlight Musicals Inc.
888 East 66th Street
P.O. Box 20152
Indianapolis, IN 46220

Star Musicals of Flint
Whiting Auditorium
1241 East Kearsley Street
Flint, MI 48502

Storrowtown Music Theatre
Eastern States Exposition Park
West Springfield, MA 01809

Totem Pole Playhouse
Caledonia State Park
Fayetteville, PA 17222

Veterans Memorial Auditorium
Columbus OH 43125

Westport Country Playhouse
25 Powers Court
Westport, CT 06880

Wolfeboro Playhouse
Box 288
Wolfeboro, NH 03894

Woodstock Performing Company
Box 511
Woodstock IL 60098

Woodstock Playhouse
P.O. Box 396
Woodstock, NY 12498

APPENDIX D

Equity Theatre for Young Audiences Companies

Allegro Productions
406 Gary Lane
Bala Cynwyd, PA 19004

American Theatre Arts for Youth
1511 Walnut Street
Philadelphia, PA 19102

Arts Mix, Inc.
(New York Committee for Young Audiences)
400 West End Avenue
New York, NY 10024

Atlanta Children's Theatre
1280 Peachtree Street, N.E.
Atlanta, GA 30309

Boston Repertory Theatre
1 Boylston Place
Boston, MA 02116

Children's Theatre Association for Young People
225 West 25th Street
Baltimore, MD 21211

Fanfare Theatre Ensemble
100 East Fourth Street
New York, NY 10003

Floating Hospital Children's Theatre
101 Park Avenue
New York, NY 10017

George Street Playhouse
414 George Street
New Brunswick, NJ 08901

Gingerbread Players & Jack
35-06 88th Street
Jackson Heights, NY 11372

Hudson Vagabond Puppets
72 Hunt Avenue
Pearl River, NY 10965

Jerz Company
100 Laurel Avenue
Kearny, NJ 07032

Just a Bunch of Us Kids
10 East 18th Street
New York, NY 10003

Kopa Kids Productions, Inc.
8 East 64th Street
New York, NY 10021

Lake Placid Center for Music, Drama, Art, Etc.
Saranac Avenue at Fawn Ridge
Lake Placid, NY 12946

Maximillion Productions
98 Riverside Drive, Apt. 7-H
New York, NY 10024

National Theatre Company
Suite 1202
165 West Sixth Street
New York, NY 10003

Performing Arts Repertory Theatre Fund, Inc.
P.O. Box 415 Cathedral Station
New York, NY 10025

Periwinkle Productions
19 Clinton Street
Monticello, NY 12701

Producers Association for Young America, Inc.
800 Third Avenue
New York, NY 10022

Rodger Hess Productions
(Bugs Bunny Follies)
509 Madison Avenue
New York, NY 10022

Stage South
c/o American Theatre Association
1029 Vermont Avenue NW
Washington, DC 20005

Wayside Theatre on Tour
Wayside Theatre
Middletown, VA 22645

Yates Musical Theatre for Children
19 Morse Avenue
East Orange, NJ 07017

Young People's Center for the Performing Arts, Inc.
228 West Houston Street
New York, NY 10014

APPENDIX E

University/Resident Theatre Association, Inc.

The following schools, universities, and theatres hold unified auditions for actors, designers, technicians, managers, directors, and theatre promoters. For more information on the National Unified Auditions write:

U/RTA Office
1540 Broadway, 10th Floor
New York, NY 10036
(212)221-1130

U/RTA Theatres
California State University—Long Beach
Department of Theatre Arts
1250 Bellflower Boulevard
Long Beach, CA 90840

Colorado Shakespeare Festival
University of Colorado
Boulder, CO 80309

Cornell University
Department of Theatre Arts
104 Lincoln Hall
Ithaca, NY 14853

Florida Atlantic University
Department of Theatre
Boca Raton, FL 33431

Florida State University
School of Theatre
Tallahassee, FL 32306

Asolo Conservatory
Florida State University
Post Office Drawer E
Sarasota, FL 33578

University of Georgia
Department of Drama
Athens, GA 30602

Harvard University
Loeb Drama Center
64 Brattle Street
Cambridge, MA 02138

University of Houston
Drama Department
Houston, TX 77004

Illinois State University
Department of Theatre
Normal, IL 61761

Indiana University
Department of Theatre and Drama
Bloomington, IN 47401

University of Iowa
Department of Speech and Dramatic Art
Iowa City, IA 52242

University of Massachusetts at Amherst
Department of Theatre
112 Fine Arts Center
Amherst, MA 01003

Memphis State University
Department of Speech and Drama
Memphis, TN 38152

Michigan State University
Performing Arts Company
Department of Theatre
East Lansing, MI 48824

University of Michigan
Professional Theatre Program
Mendelssohn Theatre
Ann Arbor, MI 48109

University of Minnesota
Department of Theatre Arts
Minneapolis, MN 55455

University of Missouri—Kansas City
Department of Theatre
5100 Rockhill Road
Kansas City, MO 64110

Montana State University
Department of Theatre Arts
Student Union Building
Bozeman, MT 59717

University of Nebraska—Lincoln
Department of Theatre Arts
University Theatre
103 Temple Building
12th and R Streets
Lincoln, NB 68508

North Dakota State University
Little Country Theatre
Fargo, ND 58102

Ohio State University
Department of Theatre
1849 Cannon Drive
Columbus, OH 43210

Oregon Shakespearean Festival Association
15 South Pioneer Street

P.O. Drawer 158
Ashland, OR 97520

Pennsylvania State University
Department of Theatre and Film
103 Arts Building
University Park, PA 16802

Purdue University
Loeb Playhouse Stewart Center
Department of Creative Arts–Theatre
West Lafayette, IN 47907

Rutgers University
Mason Gross School of the Arts
New Brunswick, NJ 08903

Santa Barbara Repertory Theatre
c/o James R. Garvin Memorial Theatre
Santa Barbara City College
721 Cliff Drive
Santa Barbara, CA 93109

Stephens College
Department of Theatre Arts
Columbia, MO 65201

State University of New York at Stony Brook
Department of Theatre Arts
Stony Brook, NY 11794

University of Texas at Austin
Department of Drama
Austin, TX 78712

Utah Shakespearean Festival
Southern Utah State College
351 West Center
Cedar City, UT 84720

Utah State University
Theatre Arts Department, UMC-40
Logan, UT 84322

University of Utah
Pioneer Memorial Theatre
Salt Lake City, UT 84112

Wayne State University
Hilberry Graduate Repertory Company
95 West Hancock
Detroit, MI 48202

Western Illinois University
Department of Theatre
Macomb, IL 61455

University of Wisconsin at Madison
University Theatre
Department of Theatre and Drama
Vilas Communication Hall
821 University Ave.
Madison, WI 53706

APPENDIX F

Outdoor Performances

The following companies produce historical dramas, classics, and musicals. Performances take place outdoors and attract audiences in the tens of thousands. Most of the companies pay full or partial staff during the summer months.

America's Witness for Christ
Bureau of Information
Hill Cumorah
Palmyra, NY 14522

Beyond the Sundown
Route 3, Box 640
Livingston, TX 77351

Blackbeard
P.O. Box 209
Bath, NC 27808

Black Hills Passion Play of America
P.O. Box 71
Lake Wales, FL 33853

Colorado Shakespeare Festival
Box Office, Campus Box 261
Colorado Shakespeare Festival

Cross and Sword
P.O. Box 1965
St. Augustine, FL 32084

Cry of the Wild Ram
P.O. Box 1792
Kodiak, AK 99615

Dust on her Petticoats
206 South Elwood
Tulsa, OK 74103

First for Freedom
Box 1776
Halifax, NC 27839

From This Day Forward
P.O. Box 112
Valdese, NC 28690

Hatfields & McCoys
P.O. Box 1205
Buckley, WV 25801

Hermannstraum
P.O. Box 461
New Ulm, MN 56073

Hernando DeSoto
P.O. Box 1259
Hot Springs, AR 71901

Horn in the West
Box 295
Boone, NC 28607

Listen and Remember
P.O. Box 1776
Waxhaw, NC 28173

Louisiana Cavalier
P.O. Box 1714
Natchitoches, LA 71457

Mountain Play Association
P.O. Box 1201
Ross, CA 94957

New Hope Musical Theatre
3801 Xylon Avenue North
New Hope, MN 55428

Oregon Shakespearean Festival
P.O. Drawer 158
Ashland, OR 97520

Ramona Outdoor Play
P.O. Box 755
Hemet, CA 92343

Sing Me No Sad Songs
P.O. Box 1355
Murfreesboro, TN 37130

Smoky Mountain Passion Play
108 1/2 Magnolia Street
Maryville, TN 37801

Song of Norway
P.O. Box 112
Mt. Horeb, WI 53572

Strike at the Wind
P.O. Box 1059
Pembroke, NC 28372

Tecumseh
P.O. Box 73
Chillicothe, OH 45601

Texas
Box 268
Canyon, TX 79015

Trail of the Lonesome Pine
Drawer 700
Big Stone Gap, VA 24219

Trumpet in the Land
P.O. Box 275
Dover, OH 44622

The Arkansaw Traveller
Box 2053
Batesville, AR 72501

The Gentleman from the Cane
P.O. Box 14
Lawrenceburg, TN 38464

The Great Passion Play
Box 471
Eureka Springs, AR 72632

The Legend of Daniel Boone
P.O. Box 365
Harrodsburg, KY 40330

The Legend of Tom Dooley
P.O. Box 24
Wilkesboro, NC 28687

The Liberty Cart
P.O. Box 470
Kenansville, NC 28349

The Little Shepherd of Kingdom Come
Box 7
Carcassonne, KY 41806

The Living Word Passion Play
Route 1
Cambridge, OH 43725

The Lone Star
P.O. Box 5253
Galveston, TX 77551

The Long Way Home
P.O. Box 711
Radford, VA 24141

The Lost Colony
P.O. Box 40
Manteo, NC 27954

The Mormon Miracle Pageant
420 A Street
Salt Lake City, UT 84103

The Mountaineer Players
719 Pike Street
Seattle, WA 98101

The Old Homestead
P.O. Box 6
East Swanzey, NH 03446

The Shepherd of the Hills
Route 1, Box 377
Branson, MO 65616

The Stephen Foster Story
P.O. Box D
Bardstown, KY 40004

The Sword of Peace
P.O. Box 535
Snow Camp, NC 27349

The Trail of Tears
P.O. Box 515
Tahlequah, OK 74464

Unto These Hills
P.O. Box 398
Cherokee, NC 28719

Utah Shakespearean Festival
351 West Center
Cedar City, UT 84720

Val Balfour's American Oberammergau Passion Play
Passion Play Garden Theatre
Strasburg, VA 22657

Where Free Men Shall Stand
125 East Queen Street
Pendleton, SC 29670

Wilderness Road
CPO 2355, Berea College
Berea, KY 40404

Wilhelm Tell
Wilhelm Tell Drama
New Glarus, WI 53574

Your Obedient Servant
P.O. Box 401
Petersburg, IL 62675

APPENDIX G

LORT Theatres

LORT stands for the League of Resident Theatres. There are LORT theatres scattered throughout the country. These companies have resident artists and administrators, and most operate on a year-round basis under a special Actors' Equity arrangement. Many young people get their start in LORT theatres.

The Acting Company
420 West 42nd Street
New York, NY 10036

Actors Theatre of Louisville
316–320 West Main Street
Louisville, KY 40202

Actors Theatre of St. Paul
2115 Summit Avenue
St. Paul, MN 55105

Alaska Repertory Theatre
523 West 8th Avenue
Anchorage, AK 99501

Alley Theatre
615 Texas Avenue
Houston, TX 77002

Alliance Theatre Company
1280 Peachtree Street NE
Atlanta, GA 30309

American Conservatory Theatre
450 Geary Street
San Francisco, CA 94102

American Revels Company of Richmond
114 West Broad Street
Richmond, VA 23220

Arizona Civic Theatre
120 West Broadway
Tucson, AZ 85701

Arena Stage
Sixth and M Streets SW
Washington DC 20024

Arrow Rock Lyceum Theatre
Arrow Rock, MO 63520

Asolo Theatre Festival
P.O. Drawer E
Sarasota, FL 33578

Barter Theatre
Abingdon, VA 24210

Bates Summer Theatre
Bates College
Lewiston, ME 04240

Berkeley Repertory Theatre
2980 College Avenue
Berkeley, CA 94705

Boston Repertory Theatre
1 Boylston Place
Boston, MA 02116

California Actors' Theatre
P.O. Box 1355
Los Gatos, CA 95030

Center for Music, Drama, and Art
Saranac Avenue at Fawn Ridge
Lake Placid, NY 12946

Center Repertory Theatre
1630 Euclid Avenue
Cleveland, OH 44115

Center Stage
700 North Calvert Street
Baltimore, MD 21202

Chelsea Theatre Center
511 West 54th Street
New York, NY 10019

Cleveland Playhouse
2040 East 86th Street
Cleveland, OH 44106

Cohoes Music Hall
58 Remsen Street
Cohoes, NY 12047

A Contemporary Theatre
709 First Avenue West
Seattle, WA 98119

Cricket Theatre
345 13th Avenue NE
Minneapolis, MN 55413

The Commonwealth Stage
Fine Arts Center
University of Massachusetts
Amherst, MA 01003

Department of Speech and Theatre
206 McClung Tower
University of Tennessee
Knoxville, TN 37916

Eugene O'Neill Memorial Theatre Center
P.O. Box 206
Waterford, CT 06385

Free Hall Theatre Company
837 Linden Street
Allentown, PA 18101

Folger Theatre Group
201 East Capitol Street SE
Washington, DC 20003

Great Lakes Shakespeare Festival
Franklin Boulevard at Bunts Road
Lakewood, OH 44107

Genesee Valley Arts Foundation
168 Clinton Avenue South
Rochester, NY 14604

Goodman Theatre Company
200 South Columbus Drive
Chicago, IL 60603

The Guthrie Theatre
725 Vineland Place
Minneapolis, MN 55403

Hartford Stage Company
50 Church Street
Hartford, CT 06103

Hartman Theatre Company
61 Atlantic Street
Stamford, CT 06901

Horse Cave Theatre
P.O. Box 215
Horse Cave, KY 42749

Illinois Theatre Center
400 Lakewood Boulevard
Park Forest, IL 60466

Indiana Repertory Theatre
411 East Michigan Avenue
Indianapolis, IN 46204

Intiman Theatre
Box 4246
Seattle, WA 98104

L.A. Free Shakespeare Festival
P.O. Box 1951
Los Angeles, CA 90028

Long Wharf Theatre
222 Sargent Drive
New Haven, CT 06520

Mark Taper Forum
Center Theatre Group
135 North Grand Avenue
Los Angeles, CA 90012

McCarter Theatre Company
P.O. Box 526
Princeton University
Princeton, NJ 08540

Meadow Brook Theatre
Oakland University
Rochester, MI 48063

Missouri Vanguard Theatre
University of Missouri at Kansas City
5100 Rockhill Road
Kansas City, MO 64110

Montana Repertory Theatre
University of Montana
Missoula, MT 59812

Milwaukee Repertory Theatre
929 North Water Street
Milwaukee WI 53202

Negro Ensemble Company
133 Second Avenue
New York, NY 10003

New Jersey Shakespeare Festival
Drew University
Madison, NJ 07940

New York Shakespeare Festival
425 Lafayette Street
New York, NY 10003

The North Light Repertory Theatre
927 Noyes
Evanston, IL 60201

Old Globe Theatre
P.O. Box 2171
San Diego, CA 92112

The Performing Arts Foundation
185 Second Street
Huntington, NY 11746

The Philadelphia Drama Guild
220 South 16th Street
Philadelphia, PA 19102

The Pittsburgh Public Theatre
300 Sixth Avenue Building
Pittsburgh, PA 15222

Players State Theatre
3500 Main Highway
Miami, FL 33133

The Playhouse Repertory Theatre
235 West 46th Street
New York, NY 10011

Playhouse in the Park
P.O. Box 6537
Cincinnati, OH 45206

Playmakers Repertory Company
103 South Building
University of North Carolina Chapel Hill
Chapel Hill, NC 27514

Repertory Theatre of Loretto-Hilton
130 Edgar Road
St. Louis, Missouri 63119

The Roundabout Theatre Company
333 West 23rd Street
New York, NY 10011

Seattle Repertory Theatre
P.O. Box B
Queen Anne Station
Seattle Center
Seattle, Washington 98109

Stage West
1511 Memorial Avenue
West Springfield, MA 01089

South Coast Repertory Theatre
655 South Town Center Drive
Costa Mesa, CA 92626

Studio Arena Theatre
710 Main Street
Buffalo, NY 14202

Syracuse Stage
820 East Genesee Street
Syracuse, NY 13210

The Advent Theatre
1202 17th Avenue South
Nashville, TN 37212

Theatre by the Sea
91 Market Street
Portsmouth, NH 03801

The Theatre at Monmouth
Cumston Hall
Monmouth, ME 04295

Trinity Square Repertory Company
201 Washington Street
Providence, RI 02903

Virginia Museum Theatre
Boulevard & Grove Avenues
Richmond, VA 22331

Bibliography

Books

Bongar, Emmet. *The Theatre Student: Practical Stage Lighting.* New York: Richards Rosen Press, 1971.
Bruder, Karl. *The Theatre Student: Properties and Dressing the Stage.* New York: Richards Rosen Press, 1969.
Cavanaugh, Jim. *The Theatre Student: Organization and Management of Nonprofessional Theatre.* Richards Rosen Press, 1973.
Cohen, Robert. *Acting Professionally.* Palo Alto: Mayfield Publishing Co., 1975.
Dance Magazine Annual '79. New York: Danad Publishing Company, 1979.
Dance Magazine College Directory. New York: Dance Magazine, 1979.
Gruver, Bert. *The Stage Manager's Handbook.* New York: Drama Book Specialists, 1973.
Kline, Peter. *The Theatre Student: Playwriting.* New York: Richards Rosen Press, 1970.
Kozelka, Paul. *The Theatre Student: Directing.* New York: Richards Rosen Press, 1968.
Langley, Stephen. *Theatre Management in America: Principle and Practice.* New York: Drama Book Specialists, 1974.
Lounsbury, Warren C. *Theatre Backstage from A to Z.* Seattle: University of Washington Press, 1972.
Musical America: 1979 International Directory of the Performing Arts. New York: ABC Leisure Magazines, 1979.
Nahas, Rebecca. *Your Acting Career.* New York: Crown Publishers, 1976.
Prisk, Berneice, and Byers, Jack A. *The Theatre Student: Costuming.* New York: Richards Rosen Press, 1970.
Rawson, Ruth. *The Theatre Student: Acting.* New York: Richards Rosen Press, 1970.
Shull, Leo. *How to Break into Show Business.* New York: Show Business Publications, 1975.

Stein, Lawrence. *Stage Management: A Guidebook of Practical Techniques.* Boston: Allyn and Bacon, 1974.
Stell, W. Joseph. *The Theatre Student: Scenery.* New York: Richards Rosen Press, 1970.
Terry, Ellen, and Anderson, Lynne. *The Theatre Student: Makeup and Masks.* New York: Richards Rosen Press, 1971.

Periodicals

Backstage, 165 West 46th Street, New York, NY 10036.
Show Business, 136 West 44th Street, New York, NY 10016.
Theatre Crafts, Rodale Press, 33 East Minor Street, Emmaus, PA 18049.